Sr. Angela spoke — a doctor and a religious sister. Recommended by Frank Spicer

Mary Cansel
703.919.3253

To Mary,
I pray that Our Lady is a LIGHT in your path.
S. Ángel de Fatima

12.ᵗʰ Mar. 2022

Inside the Light

INSIDE
THE LIGHT

Understanding the Message of Fatima

Sr. Angela de Fatima Coelho

TAN Books
Gastonia, North Carolina

Cover design by Caroline Green

Cover image © 2020 Aliança de Santa Maria

Library of Congress Control Number: 2020940003

ISBN: 978-1-5051-1607-6
Kindle ISBN: 978-1-5051-1608-3
EPUB ISBN: 978-1-5051-1609-0

Published in the United States by
TAN Books
PO Box 269
Gastonia, NC 28053
www.TANBooks.com

Printed in the United States of America

Dedicated to the Immaculate Heart of Mary

Contents

Foreword

When a family friend invited me to a Fatima retreat being given by Sister Angela Coelho on the campus of Belmont Abbey College in March of 2019, hopeful that her talks could be turned into the book you presently hold, I had a certain expectation of who might await me.

Since she was a sister of the Aliança de Santa Maria, who live in Portugal and help to spread the Fatima message, and since she had worked on the cause for canonization of the three shepherd children, I immediately pictured a soft-spoken, elderly, and reserved woman—rather like a three-dimensional version of an image from a stained glass window.

She quickly put all my preconceptions to flight when, not ten minutes into her first talk, she was talking about the NBA! God certainly loves to surprise us.

The first thing you notice about Sister Angela is her vibrancy. She is not elderly at all, but even if she were, she would have more energy than a kindergartener on the playground. Her winsome personality makes it seem as though she is walking several feet off the air, and she takes delight in sweeping you along for the ride, no matter if you are prepared for it or not. Perhaps you know people like this, whose happiness is so contagious you can *feel* it burning in your heart. This energy she exuded despite being jetlagged and giving talks that lasted several hours across multiple days.

And yes, she did talk about going to her first NBA game. That had happened the night before, a dream from long ago finally realized (she grew up watching games in Portugal with her brother). This was a small detail from her presentations, but it stuck with me as a young man who loves sports. It made me realize holiness is not hidden in the clouds. It's nearby. Among us. Within reach. It's possible to like basketball and be holy. Who knew?

Another quality that stands out is Sister Angela's humour. She had everyone rolling with laughter, people of all ages, races, and nationalities, lay and religious alike. She knows how to tell a good story, is self-deprecating without a hint of false pride, and has a charming Portuguese accent that makes admirable and charming attempts at English expressions, often without success.

Oh yeah, one more thing . . . she's also a doctor. Yes, you read that right. A religious sister *and* a doctor. How many people can tend to the health of your body and your soul all in one check-up?

You'll soon come to learn Sister Angela's story, how it has been woven up with Fatima since she was a little girl, and how she walked this path to both medical school and her religious vows, the latter of which led her to overseeing the canonization process of the shepherd children. But for now, my own personal interaction with her can give you a glimpse into who she is.

When I eventually got to spend some time with her, she immediately said she knew who I was because she had been praying for my youngest child. At first, I was dumbfounded as to why she would be doing this. Then it came back to me. My two-month-old had experienced a scary episode of

RSV (respiratory syncytial virus) some months prior, and a family friend had asked Sister Angela to pray for her. I was nearly moved to tears that she, who probably received dozens, if not hundreds, of prayer requests a day, would pray for a young child whom she had never met on the other side of the world, not to mention remembering to ask about her months later.

Later that day, the conference held a Mass, which my wife and children attended. After the celebration, we asked for a picture with her, which she graciously agreed to. But she said it would be better to take it outside, so she grabbed two of my daughters' hands and ushered them out of the church, talking to them and making them smile. This may seem a small thing, but if you knew how shy my children were, you would know it was no small thing at all. They hesitated *not for a second* to receive her hand and walk with her, leaving mommy and daddy behind. Children can sense goodness.

We took our picture and then my family departed, leaving me some time to discuss this book with Sister. We agreed it would not be an easy process, her attempting to write a book in English and me trying to help her—all with the Atlantic between us—but we both felt it was worth the effort. Her life's work is to spread the message of Fatima, and this was a great opportunity to do it.

I will not go into detail about the content of her talks, for that is the purpose of this book, but some brief prefatory comments about Fatima could serve us well.

Most would acknowledge that the apparitions of the Virgin Mary at Fatima have long fascinated Catholics and non-Catholics alike. These apparitions are of great importance for many individually and spiritually, but the words of Our Lady at Fatima are also a message for our time and to our world. She spoke not only about the necessity for personal holiness but also about the role each individual can play in changing history by helping to change our culture, our world, and the Church. As such, the apparitions at Fatima have a claim on everyone's interest, since the message communicated there is both personal and universal.

There are elements in these accounts that appeal to a wide variety of readers. For those interested in religion, the Fatima message offers a treasure trove of theological, prophetic, mystical, and devotional insights. The spiritual riches to be gleaned on the Rosary, reparation for sins, the Eucharist, the Trinity, and God's love for humanity are enough to last more than several lifetimes.

But there is also much to interest those who are not primarily students of theology. There is the fascinating, repeated miraculous presence of the Mother of God. There is the initial appearance of an angel, and subsequently, of Jesus and St. Joseph. And there is Our Lady's expression of her loving care for God's children and her assurance of God's love for each of us.

The Fatima story also features Our Lady's prophecies, a startling vision of hell, warnings about the geopolitical disasters that would ensue if humans did not turn back to God, and the amazing miracle of the sun—witnessed by as many as seventy thousand people. As if this were not enough, there is also the famous three-part "secret" revealed by the Virgin Mary at Fatima that would have significant consequences for the Church and the world. We will embark on these storylines and more shortly.

We will also soon meet the three main characters of this story, the three young, illiterate shepherd children who lived in an out-of-the-way village in Portugal a hundred years ago, when World War I was tearing Europe apart. Two of these children—Francisco and Jacinta—would become the youngest non-martyred saints in Church history, not simply because they saw the Virgin Mary but because they lived the message she delivered to them back in 1917 so fully and so perfectly.

Of course, the other figures in the story are all of us, who certainly have been affected by many of the events about which Our Lady warned: the Second World War, the spread of the Soviet Union's godless atheism, and the evident discord and trouble throughout the modern world and in the Church.

Clearly, from numerous perspectives, Fatima has always had claim on our interest, but now, a little more than one hundred years after the first apparition, the message of Fatima is particularly relevant to our times and to the spiritual and global situation in which we find ourselves. It is obviously time to re-assess the Fatima message, to put it in its full theological context, and to understand the gamut of spiritual riches that this message contains.

For Sister Angela, Fatima is more than a place, a topic of great spiritual and intellectual interest, and the subject of her talks. Fatima is more even than the source of her vocation, the charism of her congregation, and her home. It is also a path to knowledge and holiness, a path to personal sanctification that she wants to share with as many people as possible.

Sister Angela has titled her book *Inside the Light*, and she shows that the light generated from the apparitions at Fatima is very great indeed. However, this book could have been called, with equally good reason, *Encounters in Love*, because Fatima is also a school for love in which we learn how much each of the Persons of the Trinity and Our Lady love us and in which Our Lady teaches us how to live in that love. Having studied, been steeped in, and lived the mystery of Fatima for many years, Sister Angela invites each of us to step forward into the Light and Love that still radiates from the small Portuguese town where Our Lady first appeared to Francisco, Jacinta, and Lucia.

As of 2017, Francisco and Jacinta, partly through Sister Angela's hard work, were canonized saints, and Lucia was named "Servant of God," a step toward the process of canonization. Through the apparitions at Fatima, God worked wonders in the lives of these three shepherd children, helping them to embark on the path to sainthood. As Sister Angela makes clear here in this book, that is a path that Our Lady encourages all of us to walk as well.

There may be no person on earth better qualified and with more knowledge of this story and the holy children who lived it than Sister Angela. But what struck me is not so much the knowledge she possesses but the *devotion* she has to Fatima. This woman is truly in love with Our Lady and her Son. May she pass on this love and devotion to you in the pages that follow.

Brian Kennelly
TAN Books

Fatima: A Review

The primary goal of this book is to take each of us deeper into the theological message of Fatima and the spirituality of the shepherd children, with the explicit goal of deepening our relationship with Christ. To keep from getting bogged down in facts, dates, and events, Sister Angela presumes a certain level of familiarity and avoids a chronological retelling of what happened. Her goal is not to relay the details of the "event" of Fatima but to go deeper into the theological and salvific message this event propagated.

If you already know the fundamental story of Fatima, we invite you to skip this section and go straight to Sister Angela's riveting introduction, where she describes her first meeting with Sister Lucia.

If, however, you are new to Fatima, it might be helpful to read this brief review, which chronicles all the key characters and events. If you would like to know more specifics, you can find a treasury of information online.

***

Fatima is a small village town in a hilly region of central Portugal on the edge of the Serra de Aire Mountains. There would be no reason for anyone to know or care about Fatima if it were not for the astonishing events that transpired there over the course of 1916 and 1917.

The story begins with three simple shepherd children: Lucia dos Santos and her two cousins, Francisco Marto and his sister Jacinta. In the spring of 1916, when Lucia was nine, Francisco eight, and Jacinta six, an angel appeared to them on a secluded hillside where they were tending their flocks. He told them not to be afraid and revealed himself as the "Angel of Peace." He taught them a new prayer and asked that they pray it with him, assuring them that the "hearts of Jesus and Mary" were listening to their prayers.

This angel also appeared later that summer. At that time, he once again encouraged the children to pray. In addition, he asked them to make sacrifices to save sinners. The angel asked the little shepherds to offer up penances and sacrifices to console Jesus and Mary for the innumerable sins committed against the Sacred Heart of Jesus and the Immaculate Heart of Mary. In the fall of that year, the angel would appear a third time, when he gave the children Holy Communion.

They did not tell anyone about these supernatural visits, but they had a profound impact on the children and prepared them for what would happen the following year.

On May 13, 1917, while Lucia, Francisco, and Jacinta were out tending flocks and playing games in a secluded area called the Cova da Iria, they noticed what seemed like a sudden storm and flash of lightning. The two girls saw a woman "more brilliant than the sun" resting over a small tree, but at first, Francisco saw nothing; only once he started praying the Rosary were his eyes opened. This woman would eventually reveal herself to be the Mother of God, but she specifically called herself "Our Lady of the Rosary" (and is also commonly referred to today as Our Lady of Fatima). But on this first visit, she did not give her name. She simply said she was from heaven and asked that the children return to this same spot five more times on the same day and time in each of the following months.

Lucia warned her cousins not to say anything about what they'd seen, but little Jacinta, unable to contain her excitement, immediately told her mother, and the news quickly spread around the town. Some people believed the children while others scoffed. Lucia's mother fell into this latter group, considering her daughter a liar. This would become a great source of pain for Lucia.

Nonetheless, the children obeyed the Lady and returned to the Cova da Iria on June 13, when she appeared to them again. A small group of people came with them but could see nothing. Lucia asked Our Lady if she would take her, Francisco, and Jacinta to heaven. Mary replied that she would take Francisco and Jacinta very soon but that Lucia would remain behind. Our Lady told Lucia that God wanted to establish devotion to the Immaculate Heart and that Lucia would be an instrument to make this happen. During this visit, the Blessed Mother also asked the children to pray the Rosary every day.

The following month—July 13—was perhaps the most dramatic visit, when Our Lady revealed the famous three-part "secret" of Fatima. After telling the children again to pray the Rosary and make sacrifices for sinners, she promised to tell them who she was in October, when she said she would perform a miracle for all to see, to help verify the shepherds' stories. She then showed the children a violent image of hell and told them that many souls were being lost not only because of their own immorality but because there was no one to pray and make sacrifices for them. To save them, she told the children to pray and offer sacrifices, encouraging them to develop a compassionate heart for sinners. Finally, she said that God wanted to establish devotion to her Immaculate Heart. This was the first part.

In the second part of the secret, she said that World War I, raging across Europe at the time, would end but that a worse war would break out if people did not stop offending God. Our Lady said that she would return at a later date and ask for the consecration of Russia to her Immaculate Heart and for the Communion of Reparation on the First Saturdays. If her requests were heeded, she prophesied that there would be peace, but if not, Russia would spread her errors throughout the world.

Finally, in the third part of the secret, Our Lady showed them yet another vision that predicted the suffering of the Church and the persecution of the "bishop dressed in white," the Holy Father, who, in the vision, was shot by legions of soldiers with bullets and arrows.

News that the children had been told a "secret" spread around town, and the local authorities demanded that its contents be revealed. Things reached such a fever pitch that the administrator of the town actually imprisoned them, keeping them from meeting Our Lady on August 13. He even threatened them with death if they did not reveal the secret. But the children stood firm and would not betray Our Lady's trust.

Eventually, after they were released, Mary appeared to them again, this time on the nineteenth of the month. She once again asked them to pray the Rosary and said there would still be a miracle in October, but it would not be as extraordinary as it would have been if the local authorities had not imprisoned the children and threatened them with death.

With each visit, the number of people accompanying the children to the site of the apparitions grew, and in September, there were so many people that the children struggled to reach the Cova da Iria. Our Lady appeared again and told them God was pleased with their sacrifices. She also said that the following month, when the promised miracle would occur, Our Lord would come, and that she would appear as Our Lady of Sorrows and Our Lady of Mount Carmel. She foretold that St. Joseph would also appear with the Child Jesus to bless the world.

Finally, October 13 came. More than seventy thousand people showed up to see the miracle, including many non-believers, some of whom worked for news and media outlets hoping to debunk the children's story and embarrass those who believed.

The weather was dire all morning and the fields were soaked in rain and mud. When Our Lady appeared, she finally told the children her name, identifying herself as Our Lady of the Rosary. She told the children she wanted a chapel built in her honor in the place where she had appeared. She pleaded with them on behalf of humanity to stop offending God, who was already gravely offended by the world's sins. She then ascended, and as promised, Our Lady of Carmel and Our Lady of Dolores appeared, as well as St. Joseph and the Child Jesus, who blessed the world.

The sun then grew brighter and began to spin and emit vivid colors before dropping to the earth. The thousands present screamed in terror. People cried out for mercy, thinking it was the end of the world. Yet a moment later, the sun resumed its normal position. When the uproar calmed down, all who were there noticed that the ground had dried and people's clothes were no longer muddy and wet. This event, which came to be known as the miracle of the sun, was seen by people for miles around. As a result of this miracle, many non-believers came to believe and converted to Christianity.

After this, the children struggled to live a normal life, often being swarmed by crowds. For Francisco and Jacinta, however, this life in the limelight would not last long. Our Lady had promised to take them to heaven soon, and indeed, both of them were stricken by the Spanish flu epidemic of 1918. Francisco died on April 4, 1919. Meanwhile, Jacinta was moved to a hospital several miles away. But she told the doctors and her family that she was going to die and that their efforts to save her would be futile. Her prophecy was fulfilled when she died on February 20, 1920 in Lisbon.

Lucia was grief-stricken not just because she had lost her cousins but because she had also lost the only two people in the world with whom she had shared the apparitions of Fatima. Many people continued to seek out Lucia, some coming from far away to see her. The local bishop recommended that she leave for Porto, where she could avoid the crowds and attend a special school. She did not want to leave Fatima, but when she visited the Cova da Iria on June 15,

1921, Our Lady appeared to Lucia for a seventh time and assured her it was God's will for her to go to Porto.

After several years spent studying in Porto, Lucia entered the Institute of the Sisters of St. Dorothy as a postulant in a convent in Pontevedra, Spain, on October 24, 1925. Just a few months later on December 10, Our Lady fulfilled her promise of coming again—appearing to Lucia in the Dorothean convent. On this visit, Mary explained the specific requirements for the Communion of Reparation on First Saturdays. In another visit in Tui, four years later in 1929, Our Lady appeared alongside a visible presence of the Most Holy Trinity and asked for the consecration of Russia to her Immaculate Heart.

Though Lucia had taken her final vows in 1934 to become a Dorothean sister, she was later released from these vows so she could become a Carmelite sister in 1948. During this period, Our Lady's prediction of a worse worldwide conflict came to pass with the outbreak of World War II. Lucia felt the pain of this war most acutely, feeling a strong personal responsibility to pray for peace. She spent the rest of her life trying to spread devotion to the Immaculate Heart of Mary and imploring people to pray the Rosary and embrace a spirituality of reparation. Under holy obedience, she was directed to record all that had happened to her and all that Our Lady had told her, which we find today in several different books (though the contents of the secret were only released to the pope and special members of the Magisterium for some time, not being released to the general public until much later).

Over the years, Lucia also met with several popes, urging them to consecrate Russia to Our Lady, according to what she had specified. Though several holy fathers tried to make this consecration, confusion and unforeseen circumstances prevented it from taking place. One specific area of confusion concerned the consecration being made in union with the bishops around the world, which failed to happen on several occasions.

This all took place amidst the backdrop of the Cold War, when the atheististic Soviet Union began a systematic takeover of Eastern Europe and became embroiled in a nucular arms race with the United States.

St. John Paul II, one of the popes most devoted to the Blessed Mother, and who had grown up under Soviet oppression in Poland, would play a significant role in the Fatima story. On May 13, 1981, on the anniversary of Our Lady's first apparition to the children, he was shot in St. Peter's Square by Mehemet Ali Agca, a Turkish man with unclear motives. John Paul credited Our Lady of Fatima with saving his life. While recovering, he read Lucia's words about the secret, specifically about the "bishop dressed in white" being shot. This obviously resonated with him, and he became determined to fulfill Our Lady's request to consecrate Russia to her Immaculate Heart. Though it took several tries, he was able to accomplish this on March 25, 1984, in front of 250,000 people in Rome. Lucia gave credence to this attempt by assuring everyone that heaven had finally accepted the consecration.

In the years that followed, Communist Russia began to collapse, symbolically illustrated by the dramatic fall of the

Berlin Wall in 1989. Though many factors no doubt contributed to this outcome, believers pointed to the consecration as a divine aid in defeating the Soviet Union, which had been the globe's leading atheistic world power.

Lucia herself saw the turn of the millennium, dying on February 13, 2005, at the age of ninety-seven. Her cause for canonization is still ongoing at the time of this writing, but her cousins, Jacinta and Francisco, were canonized on May 13, 2017, the hundredth anniversary of Our Lady's first apparition at the Cova da Iria. Today, millions seek their intercession and practice a strong devotion to Our Lady of Fatima.

Meeting Lucia

Some encounters permanently mark our lives, even though we do not always perceive them as such while living them. My first meeting with Sister Lucia de Jesus, one of the shepherd children of Fatima, was like that.

I like to drive. But on that day, March 28, 2001, my anxiety was greater than my fondness for driving. In the drizzling rain, the car wound its way through the streets of Coimbra toward the Carmelite Convent of Saint Therese. My heart suspected that this woman was about to change my life, though to the degree that she would change it, I did not yet know.

The previous day, Father Kondor, the vice postulator for Francisco and Jacinta Marto's cause for canonization, had invited me to go to the convent to sing happy birthday to Sister Lucia. It was her ninety-fourth!

What Sister Lucia had witnessed in Fatima and what she had taught the world in the decades following had shaped the charism of my religious vocation and my apostolic mission. My life was mysteriously linked to hers, although she did not know it and I had not yet grasped the extent to which this would be the case. Being just hours away from seeing her, listening to her, talking to her . . . touching

1

her . . . was surreal. I was so excited that I could not sleep a wink the night before.

When we arrived at the Carmelite convent where Sister Lucia lived, Father Kondor and I entered into a kind of lobby or greeting room. It was simple and austere, with light filtering in from one small window on the right. The room was full of other guests who would help celebrate Sister Lucia's birthday. Looking them over, I wondered what each of them had in their hearts, what wish or hope they held, what words they hoped to hear from Lucia. Maybe some of them, like me, were eager to meet the woman who—over eight decades ago—had seen a bit of heaven.

Finally, Sister Lucia arrived. She was tiny and obviously very old, yet she brought so much light! Her life, which we were commemorating that day, was a bright dialogue with the Holy Trinity—Light Itself. In that dialogue, Lucia had opened herself up to grace and to be transformed by the action of the Spirit. In the more than eighty years since the apparitions, Lucia's whole life had been an effort to become more like Christ, whom she had learned to know and love through the Immaculate Heart of Mary. As all of us looked at Lucia, we saw that she had become a reflection of that divine brightness.

As she moved throughout the room, Lucia eventually came my way. When she looked at me—what a look!—I swallowed my nerves and said, "Sister Lucia, I belong to a religious community, the Alliance of Holy Mary. Our charism is to continue the Little Shepherds' mission, to share the message of Fatima, and to spread devotion to the Immaculate Heart of Mary."

Sister Lucia immediately replied with an unexpected charm that captivated me, "Then you have to come to the Carmelite Convent . . . it's where I am."

Surprised by this good-natured response, I immediately felt more at ease. I smiled and replied, "Sister, I cannot come here to stay. I already have my vocation and I need to continue spreading the angel's and Our Lady's requests *in Fatima*."

Lucia returned my smile as she silently gazed at me then said, "And Our Lady is pleased with that." I cannot express how encouraging these simple words were, and I thank the Lord for this meeting still to this day.

Over the next three years, I met Sister Lucia four more times. Although brief, our meetings always left me with a feeling of peace and a sense of her great simplicity. She was a woman completely given over to God, which has a way of ironing out the complexities of our human nature.

On one of our visits, I was touched by her lasting faithfulness to the "yes" she had given Our Lady on May 13, 1917. Lucia didn't just say yes to Our Lady that day, she clearly had said it every day of her life after that.

Sometime later, several years after Lucia had died, on May 13, 2010, when Pope Benedict XVI came to Fatima, he beautifully described the meaning of Lucia's "yes": "Faithfulness over time is the name of love."[1] When I heard him say these words, I immediately remembered Sister Lucia and our conversation on a pleasant spring evening in 2004. At the end of that meeting, as I was saying goodbye, I held out

---

[1]   Benedict XVI, May 12, 2010, Fátima, Celebration of Vespers with the Priests, Religious, Seminarians and Deacons.

my hands. She squeezed them between hers and said, "These hands shall enter the Carmelite Convent one day." I was silent and thought to myself, "*That* is never going to happen!" She only smiled in response to my dubious expression.

Years later, in June 2013, while in Rome and then serving as postulator of Francisco and Jacinta's cause for canonization, I met Father Romano Gambalunga, general postulator of the Carmelites. We spoke of the causes of these precious saints,[2] the Little Shepherds of Fatima. Then the following year, in September 2014, he invited me to be vice postulator of Sister Lucia's cause. It was a new way to "meet" with her, a meeting that still goes on today, mediated by her writings. These include her private diary, *O Meu Caminho* (*My Path*), her personal notes, and some letters that she wrote, as well as the testimony of those who lived with her. All of these give a fascinating insight into the inner life of Lucia de Jesus.

On February 13, 2017, at the conclusion of the diocesan stage of Sister Lucia's beatification and canonization process, Mother Celina, prioress of the Coimbra Carmelite Convent, invited me to visit Sister Lucia's cell. This moved me to tears! Mother Celina let me sit on Sister Lucia's bed, and it was then that I remembered her words: "These hands shall enter the Carmelite Convent one day!" Sister Lucia was right. It did happen. There I was in the Carmelite Convent where the servant of God, Lucia de Jesus, lived and wrote so many

---

[2]   Francisco and Jacinta were canonized by Pope Francis on May 13, 2017, in Fatima. As to the Servant of God Lucia de Jesus, as of the writing of this book, her process is already in the Roman stage. The author does not intend, in whatever way, to get ahead of the Church's judgement with this expression.

of the documents that constitute today the process for her beatification and canonization.

What this woman experienced in the year 1917 constitutes the core of my dedication to the Lord. What this woman wrote until the end of her life, at ninety-seven, constitutes the living matter of my mission now that I work for her canonization. I would never have suspected this turn of events all those years ago when I first met her. Did Lucia know? Maybe, maybe not, but I suspect Jesus and his mother knew.

Since 1997, I have given lectures about the message of Fatima all over the world, including in the United States, several European countries, and in South America. In 2017, to celebrate the hundredth anniversary of the Fatima apparitions, the Shrine of Fatima invited me to prepare a course about the message of Fatima, one that we could give to pilgrims. This current book is derived from a vast set of theological and personal reflections that formed my lectures and courses over the last twenty years.

The objective of my talks and of this book is to help those interested in Fatima know more about the apparitions and how the message of Fatima can enrich and enhance their own lives and the life of the Church.

Where appropriate, I have cited my sources in both the text and the footnotes. I feel indebted to the many masters whom I heard and read and who helped teach me about this story. I have noted some of the writers and texts which can help others deepen their knowledge of this theme. It is possible that some passages may be found without bibliographical reference, but which were inspired there.

Of course, the primary influence on my work is Lucia, both my meetings with her and her own writings. My wish is that this book may help you come to know her and the story and message of Fatima so that you may become a greater disciple of Jesus Christ in the twenty-first century. Or perhaps said another way, my wish is that, as Lucia said, "Our Lady is pleased with this."

What immense light shone from Fatima in 1917. The world, one hundred years later, needs a light like that, so let us go inside the light!

A Life Shaped by Fatima

Growing Up in Portugal

This book is not about me. It is about Our Lady and those three precious children she visited throughout the course of 1917.

However, I feel it is necessary to give you a little background about myself and my apostolate so that you can better understand the perspective from which I tell this story. After all, when you grow up in Portugal, Fatima shapes your life in unique ways.

Jesus and Mary were a constant presence in my family's house. You might say they were *living members* of the family. My father, Manuel, and my mother, Maria do Céu, were married in 1968 in Porto.

After the wedding celebration, they went to Fatima. In the Chapel of the Apparitions, they prayed their first Rosary as a family and dedicated their wedding to Our Lady of Fatima. They were a Catholic couple who practiced their faith in a natural way. With much simplicity, they united what they believed in to what they lived.

They had a family business in the clothing industry. Their love for God, for Our Lady, for family, and for hard, honest work were their trademarks, and they passed this on to all their children. Our parents were charitable and keenly aware of the importance of sharing what they had with the poor and needy. This helped us to imitate their generosity and to understand that giving is a source of joy.

My father constructed a small "chapel" in our house where we gathered at the end of the day to pray the Rosary as a family. I remember the stained-glass with the face of Jesus, the beautiful crucifix, and, of course, Our Lady of Fatima's statue, which rested to the left of the small altar. My father liked to kneel down before the Virgin of the Rosary's statue. That was his place, in the family and in life: at the feet of Our Lady, his hands clutching his rosary, *her* rosary.

I have many memories of that time with my family. I do not know if, at that time, those of us who were the youngest actually prayed much. As soon as the prayers started, we would go to our grandmother's lap or to one of our two aunts who lived with us. I believe that we fell asleep before getting to the second mystery, but as if by magic, we woke up at the Hail Holy Queen.

On April 1, 1978, my father and mother, with all members of the family (four children, two aunts, a cousin, and our grandmother), consecrated the family at the end of a Holy Mass, as well as our properties and time, to the Immaculate Heart of Mary. This was in accordance to the spirit of the message of Fatima and of the apparition of the Holy Trinity and of Our Lady to Lucia in Tui, which took place on June 13, 1929.

In my childish spirituality, I was absolutely sure that this consecration would put our whole family under the special protection of Mary and that no harm would come to any of us.

A Time of Suffering

Two years later, on January 5, 1980, my sister, Maria Goretti, not even three years old, suffered a domestic accident and died the next day. I cannot describe the sadness in my parents' eyes, and I shall never forget her small, lifeless body. I was eight years old and this was my first contact with death.

Although I was not able to express what I was feeling, I know that it was the first time I started to doubt the "absolute" protection of God and Our Lady and about what it might mean to be under their care. At Christmas that year, my parents told us that my mother was pregnant. The joy of a new life helped to mitigate the loss of my little sister, but obviously, her death still hung over all of us like a storm cloud.

The following year, on February 14, 1981, my parents travelled on business to Spain. On that fateful day, my father lost his life in a terrible road accident. My mother, who returned home a widow and pregnant with my youngest sister, was never the same. The anguish, the helplessness, the doubts and fear for the future darkened her eyes and took away her joy. She was alone, still young—forty-four years old—with five children and a business with more than sixty employees. In a little more than a year, she had lost a daughter and her husband.

For the next five years, blackness covered our home and our spirits—in the clothes, in the darkness of our eyes, in the conversations, in the silences, in the absence of joy when playing, and even in praying, which we continued to do.

In order to not increase my mother's pain, I kept my deep doubts concerning faith to myself, which became the ever-present backdrop of my spiritual life. After all, what good had come from my family's consecration to Our Lady? Shouldn't this consecration have put us under Jesus's special protection? It seemed that our life had been idyllic until then. Only after the consecration did the deaths and losses begin. Fear surrounded my future and I struggled with insecurities and a deep sadness.

Since I didn't share my doubts and problems with anyone, no one was able to explain that the consecration to Our Lady does not confer magical protection from any pain or difficulty, give the assurance of perpetual happiness, or ensure a problem-free existence. I gave no one the opportunity to explain that such a dedication does not prevent us suffering but gives us the assurance of God's and Our Lady's special presence with us. The consecration assures that they will accompany us, suffer with us, and help us to bear our suffering.

I was too young to understand any of this. The image of an almighty God, a Father, always and only kind, who listens to our prayers, watching over our lives and protecting us, was ruined for me. I still believed in God but felt that he did not care about us.

Only many years later, when I was already a nun, was I able to start purifying the wrong image of God that I had built up as a result of the losses and emotional wounds I suffered as a child. Only many years later, reinterpreting my life in the light of the Fatima mystery, was I able to understand the deep meaning of the losses my family had suffered.

To avoid causing my mother any more pain, I hid the debris of my inner spiritual earthquake. I maintained the appearance of a religiosity through external rituals, going to Mass and praying the Rosary with the family at the end of each day, but inside it was only dryness and bitterness. It was a very dark time from which I likely would never have emerged if not for my mother's unshakable faith.

Perhaps it was my mother's faith and her maternal love that caused my relationship with Our Lady to remain relatively unaffected. I felt that God was "responsible" for the tragedies that had happened, or at least was responsible for not having protected us from them. Mary, on the other hand, I felt was not responsible. Feeling close to her made me also feel closer to my father, for I knew he was with her.

Today, I am aware that Our Lady was the instrument God used to keep me close to him, like a blanket that wrapped me up with him even though I was trying to wrestle myself away. It would take more than twenty years for my anger to pacify, allowing Jesus to return to my heart again, when I could say with St. Paul, "We know that in everything God works for good with those who love him, who are called according to his purpose" (Rom 8:28).

The Alliance of Holy Mary

Our family eventually decided to move to Porto, Portugal's second largest city, approximately sixty miles from the village where I had grown up. My mother moved us because we would have more educational opportunities in Porto and my mother, who had been a primary teacher years earlier, would be able to teach again. With my father gone, our family business had been shut down, so it was necessary for my mother to return to teaching to provide for our livelihood.

At this stage, my mother rekindled a relationship with her best friend from university, Maria Clara, who, with another woman named Maria Aurea, was starting a life of religious consecration. They were a small community of lay people who would later become known as the Alliance of Holy Mary.

Maria Aurea was a high school art teacher when she met Maria Clara, who was training to be an elementary school teacher. Women of unusual intelligence and strength of will, but with quite different origins and personalities, they sought to follow Christ faithfully. Finding in each other the same impulse of the Holy Spirit and a great shared love for Our Lady, they felt called to a life of prayer, consecration, and communion with God through the hands of the Immaculate Heart of Mary. In 1966, forty-one-year-old Aurea and nineteen-year-old Clara left everything and embarked upon their life-long mission of spreading the message of Fatima.

At that time in Portugal, devotion to Our Lady of Fatima was alive in the hearts of the people. Many visited the shrine and prayed the Rosary daily in their homes. However, for the most part, devotion to Our Lady of Fatima was expressed only in fragmented devotional practices, without any link to the mysteries of Jesus Christ. There was a lack of knowledge of the Fatima message's theological dimension. Furthermore, in this period, sometimes even called the "decade without Mary,"[3] the Portuguese hierarchy tended to regard Fatima with suspicion and detachment, relegating it to the sphere of popular religion.

The founders of the Alliance of Holy Mary[4] felt that the message of Fatima, having been a gift granted by God to the Church and to the world, was being neglected. They felt it was their responsibility, as well as that of the Portuguese people, to make the message more widely known and, perhaps just as important, *better understood.* They intensified the apostolic work of spreading the practice of praying the Rosary, as well as the requests from Our Lady for reparation and consecration. From this renewed mission sprouted lay movements linked to the congregation: the National Rosary Crusade and Luminaries of Holy Mary,[5] to name a few.

Under the banner of "prayer and contemplation," consecrated in poverty, chastity, obedience, and unity, each congregation member sought to grow in holiness through the

---

[3]   A misinterpretation of a chapter dedicated to Our Lady in *Lumen gentium* helped to promote this unfortunate situation. *Lumen gentium,* which is a dogmatic constitution on the Church, was promulgated by Pope Paul VI in 1964. In Portugal, this misinterpretation caused a decrease in the Church's promotion of devotion to the Virgin Mary. Some authors actually thought that Vatican Council II (1962-1965) had put a stop to that devotion. Consequently, there was the so-called "decade without Mary" (1964–1974), an expression that is perhaps a little hyperbolic.

[4]   You may consult more data on this religious Congregation at www.aliancadesantamaria.com.

[5]   With the first approval from the Diocese of Arlington, Virginia on July 16, 2014, these groups started to grow, and at this moment, they are present in Arlington, Virginia, Charlotte, North Carolina, and Fort Wayne and South Bend, Indiana.

Immaculate Heart of Mary. Their charism, therefore, drank from the fountain of the message of Fatima.

The Alliance movement was approved as an Association of the Faithful in the Archdiocese of Braga on November 28, 1985. The statute of Religious Congregation, with respective canonical institution, was achieved on June 13, 2002, and approved by the archbishop of Braga. Presently, its members are spread out in five Portuguese dioceses across six communities.

This was the community that would slowly begin to change my life. My encounters with them began in a small apartment in Porto where they had lived since the mid-seventies. Every first Saturday of the month, in accordance with the request Our Lord and Our Lady made to Sister Lucia (on December 10, 1925 in Pontevedra), Maria Aurea and Maria Clara organized a meeting in their home where they gathered families and friends, guiding them in the First Saturdays' program.

My family started to attend these gatherings on the first Saturday of each month. Maria Clara prayed the Rosary with the children and teenagers and guided them in the fifteen minutes of meditation on the Gospel requested by Jesus and Our Lady. These meditations would be on one of the mysteries of the Rosary. All this was followed by confession and Mass, which we, in accord with Our Lady's request, offered in reparation to the Immaculate Heart of Mary.

At that time, I certainly did not understand everything in the message of Fatima, especially the concept of making reparation. But I was always very happy to go, if for no other reason than the tea time at the end, when I ate more than my share of delicious refreshments. The sisters prepared everything with such care that, I confess, it was not so much love for Our Lady but the expectation of those home-baked cookies that ensured my monthly attendance at these events!

Month after month, year after year, we attended the meetings at the sisters' house. I loved the joy they radiated. Their love for the Eucharist and for the message of Fatima was contagious, as was their diligence in spreading devotion to the Immaculate Heart of Mary. I was especially delighted when I perceived the effect that these spiritual meetings were having on my mother. Slowly, she regained her joy through time spent with these sisters and at their holy gatherings.

Gradually, I myself began to perceive a desire to "be like them." Years earlier, when I was still a child and my mother was pregnant with one of my sisters, I had decided to be a doctor to "take the baby out of my mummy's tummy." Now, I wanted to be a nun!

Doctor and nun. This would be my life. I told this to my mother, who thought, "Ah, kids!"

The idea of becoming a nun, however, gradually disappeared, and at the age of eighteen, in 1989, I was admitted to the Faculty of Medicine at the University of Porto. Even though I might have forgotten about being a nun, God seemed to have remembered.

Amidst many doubts and difficulties, it appeared that he wanted me for the religious life. His providence brought the sisters of the Alliance of Holy Mary back into my life some years later. When I was with them, I felt drawn to their charism and to becoming a nun. Helped by their guidance, I discerned that this was God's will for me. I decided that

I would become a member of the Alliance of Holy Mary, working to promote the message of Fatima.

I didn't understand much about the spiritual life but trusted in Our Lady. After all, I had already learned that we do not understand everything right away. If we wait for perfect understanding each time we set out to satisfy the will of God, we will never do anything at all. Trust must come first, followed by understanding.

During my time in the Faculty of Medicine, I had many vocational crises. In fact, I had so many, I believe I became an expert in vocational crises!

Nonetheless, on July 16, 1995, one week after my last medicine exam, I joined the Alliance of Holy Mary. I had dreamt of entering on a date related to the message of Fatima, but I joined on the feast day of Our Lady of Mount Carmel. Of course, this date would take on more meaning later because of my meetings with Sister Lucia in the Carmelite Convent. In retrospect, I began to understand that it was, in fact, the right day, *my day*, the one that the Lord had prepared for me.

It seems that many of the things that happen in our lives only begin to make sense many years later. In my own life, God has certainly shown me that we must be patient and not expect to understand everything immediately. We must give God the time he wants to help us understand. He delights in showing us how he takes care of us, leading us by the hand and keeping us under his mantle, in his fatherly heart.

Becoming Postulator

After the novitiate and the juniorate time, I was appointed mistress of novices. This meant I was in charge of the formation of the new vocations for our congregation. To better carry out this mission, my community asked me to study religious sciences (what you would call theology in the States). In 2008, I finished my degree in religious sciences at the Universidad de Comillas in Madrid. As soon as I finished, a new challenge presented itself.

I had become acquainted with Father Luis Kondor, the vice postulator[6] of Blessed Francisco and Jacinta's causes, having served as his doctor. His health was very poor, and I would often travel with him to Rome on account of his fading health. During these trips, we would discuss the lives and holiness of Blessed Francisco and Jacinta, the message of Fatima, and the Immaculate Heart of Mary. On one of these trips, I was fortunate enough to meet the postulator of the little shepherds' cause, Father Paolo Molinari, SJ.

In June 2009, Father Kondor's health began to decline sharply, and he died on October 28 of that year. At that time, D. António Marto, bishop of the Leiria-Fatima diocese, asked Father Molinari to let me be Father Kondor's

---

6   Vice postulator is the person chosen by the postulator, and the author of a cause, to represent the cause of a candidate to sanctity outside Rome. The person (or group, or diocese) who wants to start a cause is the author of the cause. In the case of Francisco and Jacinta, the author was the Diocese of Leiria-Fatima, and in the case of Lucia, the author is the Carmel of Coimbra. The author chooses the postulator, but the Congregation for the Causes of Saints must approve this individual. Then the postulator chooses the vice postulator, and again the author must approve this person as well.

successor. Thus, on November 1, 2009, the Solemnity of All Saints, I became vice postulator for the causes of Blessed Francisco and Jacinta Marto.

This development confused me because I felt incapable. I thought only a priest could be postulator or vice postulator. Yet at the same time, I felt so much love for these two little shepherd saints. I knew they were, along with their cousin Lucia, there at the genesis of my community, totally devoted to the experience and diffusion of the Fatima message. So I took my new role as a sign from God; it was his will that I take on these duties.

More change would follow in 2011, when Father Molinari reached the maximum age allowed to be a postulator. He asked D. António Marto to let me become his successor. Despite my objection, on June 22, 2012, Cardinal Angelo Amato, prefect of the Congregation for the Causes of the Saints, appointed me Roman postulator of Blessed Francisco and Jacinta Marto's causes. Then, as already noted, on September 8, 2014, I was appointed vice postulator of the cause for the beatification and canonization of the Servant of God Sister Lucia.

A New Perspective

Being responsible for the causes of the three shepherd children of Fatima gave me the opportunity to study the message of Fatima more intensely. Of course, I was already familiar with the events connected to all the apparitions, but this time, I studied everything that had happened through the eyes of Francisco, Jacinta, and Lucia. Until then, my access to information about Fatima had been, like that of anyone else, through published works available to the public. Now, I was given access to private documents related to the lives of the children. It was an incredible privilege and significant responsibility.

More amazing than the knowledge of new facts, however, was the beauty of understanding how each of the children lived the message they had received, each in a different way, but fully. I was able to contemplate the mystery of Fatima through their eyes and hearts.

Without my noticing it, the deep doubts of my childhood were erased. The pain and darkness that I had experienced were transformed into something new and whole again. My memories were no longer loaded with the harrowing suffering that had marked the soul of the child I once was. On the contrary, they emerged as a prism that illuminated answers to the most difficult questions. I was able to perceive how God had led me during those years of trial and pain, how he had accompanied me in each second of despair and suffering, and how his mercy had embraced me despite all my limitations, sins, and vulnerabilities. But this is not only about me. The light of the message of Fatima has the power to heal the wounds of many others as well.

At the end of 2016 and in January and February of 2017, documents regarding all the causes of the Fatima seers sat on my desk. It made me happy to think that the three little shepherd children of Fatima were, in a sense, re-united on the desk where I worked. It was a time of hard work but also joy, seeing their causes for sainthood unfold right before me. My daily association with these holy children has strengthened my vocation in the Alliance of Holy Mary, enriched the relationship I share with the other members of the congregation, and enhanced the talks I give to pilgrims who seek to better know the message of Fatima. I also believe that those who hear about the lives of these children and their devotion inevitably grow in their own appreciation of the mystery of Fatima.

All of us associated with the causes of the three children were working simultaneously on the miracle that would lead to the canonization of Francisco and Jacinta and on the required documentation for the conclusion of the diocesan phase of the beatification and canonization process of Lucia. After several years of intense study and work, the process was complete.

May 13, 2017 eventually came, the day of the canonizations of Francisco and Jacinta. As I walked through the Shrine of Fatima, holding relics of the little shepherds, I thought back to the pain of my childhood. Then suddenly, during this huge procession, I looked back and saw the statue of Our Lady of the Rosary of Fatima. It brought to mind the meeting I had with Lucia and a profound insight that she recorded in her memoir concerning the second apparition of the Angel of Peace: "We understood who God was, how he loved us and [how he] wanted to be loved."

This is what the Blessed Virgin came to do in Fatima. She came to announce again to a world immersed in darkness and suffering that God loves each of us and wants us to love him in return.

When the procession finally reached the altar and I set the relics at the feet of Our Lady's statue, my emotions overwhelmed me. With great gratitude, I witnessed Pope Francis canonize Francisco and Jacinta Marto.

And in that moment, I sang my *Magnificat*.

CHAPTER 2

A School of Faith

"Tell Me How It Happened!"

One morning, at a time before the apparitions, Jacinta and Lucia were playing in Lucia's house. Jacinta lost the game, as usual, and as the loser, she was supposed to hug and kiss Lucia's brother.

"No, I would rather give a hug and a kiss to a crucifix hanging on the wall."

"All right," Lucia answered. "You will give three hugs and three kisses. One for you, one for Francisco, and one for me."

"To Our Lord, I will give as many as you want."

Jacinta ran quickly to the crucifix and kissed and hugged it with such devotion that Lucia would never forget it. Jacinta then asked, while gazing at Our Lord, "Why is he nailed to the cross?"

"Because he died for us."

"Tell me how it happened!" Jacinta begged.[7]

---

[7]   Lucia dos Santos, *Fatima in Lucia's Own Words* (Fátima: Fundação Francisco e Jacinta Marto, 2018), p. 39.

Tell me how it happened! What an innocent but honest (and profound) request. I would like to think of this book as a talk between myself and you, the reader, in a cozy room as I try to tell you, with Lucia's assistance, *how it all happened.*

"I Want You to Learn How to Read"

These words from Our Lady were directed to Lucia on June 13, 1917, during the second apparition.[8] What a peculiar request, one of the most remarkable and surprising things in the whole story of Fatima. This is not usually something we think of when we consider spiritual apparitions. The Blessed Mother asks for prayer, of course, but reading?

It makes sense if we think more deeply about it. Our Lady was asking for study, for knowledge, for going deeper into our faith. It is impossible to fully reach God without faith, but it is perhaps just as important to use our intellectual capacity to draw us closer to him.

Pope St. John Paul II, in his encyclical *Fides et Ratio* (*Faith and Reason*), explains this, saying, "Faith and reason are like two wings on which the human spirit rises to the contemplation of truth; and God has placed in the human heart a desire to know the truth—in a word, to know himself—so that, by knowing and loving God, men and women may also come to the fullness of truth about themselves."[9]

The Holy Father said it well: faith and human reflection are like two wings with which we fly to God. If you cut one, the soul's journey is handicapped. Faith without reason can become superstition. Reason without faith might

---

8   See ibid., p. 177.
9   John Paul II, Encyclical *Fides et Ratio*, September 14, 1998.

remain superficial and does not penetrate fully in the pursuit of truth.

This teaching of the Church's Magisterium is present in Our Lady's message at Fatima when she says, "I want you to pray the rosary and I want you to learn how to read." We must pray, yes, but we must also use our minds to go deeper. Therefore, the purpose of this book and all the effort at formation that we do is to answer one of the main requests of Our Blessed Mother.

When Our Lady asked for this, she was referring more to Lucia than to Francisco and Jacinta, who would die within a few years. Lucia's mission was to spread word of the great love that God has towards humanity. In order to do this, she needed to be able to read and write. This may sound like a simple thing, but in 1917 Portugal, girls were not generally schooled, especially in poorer areas like Fatima. It was not an easy request to fulfill. Nonetheless, Lucia would go on to fulfill it, as we will see.

We must admit that we, Catholics of the twenty-first century, with access to so much information, often neglect our Christian formation. Perhaps we say we don't have the time, or maybe it's just a lack of interest. But the words of St. Peter apply to us as much as to the earliest Christians: "Always be prepared to make a defense to anyone who calls you to account for the hope that is in you" (1 Pt 3:15).

The story of Fatima is very much about love and faith, but there is a rich theology underlying the message of Our Lady. We must *study* the story as much as *listen* to it, and only then can we *understand* it, and then *live* it! I applaud you for taking the time to go deeper. So now let us enter Our Lady's classroom!

Mary, Our Teacher

When the Portuguese Episcopal Conference went to the Vatican in November of 2007, Pope Benedict XVI surprised many when he dedicated the last part of his talk to Fatima. "I am pleased to think of Fatima as a school of faith with the Virgin Mary as the teacher; there she established her 'chair' to teach the young visionaries, and then the multitudes, the eternal truths and the art of praying, believing and loving. With the humble attitude of students who need to learn the lesson, entrust daily to the illustrious Teacher and the Mother of the whole Christ each one of you."[10]

As we know, Pope Benedict XVI was a man who measured his words very carefully. It should catch our attention, then, that he, who sat on the *Chair of Peter*, says that, in Fatima, Our Lady established her *chair*. With this he means that in Fatima, Our Lady is truly a teacher of the Catholic Church, where she teaches the eternal truths of the Faith and the art of praying, believing, and loving.

The advice of our emeritus pope is this: if there is anyone who thinks he or she still needs to learn how to love, Fatima is the school in which they can learn. If there is anyone who thinks he or she still needs to learn how to pray a little bit better, Fatima is the school in which they can learn. If there is anyone who thinks he or she still needs to increase in faith, Fatima is the school in which they can learn.

---

[10]   Benedict XVI, address to members of the Episcopal Conference of Portugal on their "ad limina" visit, November 10, 2007.

Is this not all of us? Of course it is!

So let us entrust ourselves to this great teacher with "the humble attitude of students who need to learn the lesson." Let us learn the lessons the Mother of God wishes to teach us concerning our growth in faith, hope, and love.

Removing the Veil

In order to benefit fully from the message of Fatima, we must first understand its theological context. One of the important theological issues the apparitions at Fatima raises is the difference between the way the Church considers *public* and *private* revelation.

Imagine a beautiful young woman standing on the stage of a big theatre. Her face is covered by a veil that she gradually removes, allowing some features of her face to show, little by little, until eventually the whole veil is removed and we can contemplate the whole of her face and the splendor of her beauty.

Now imagine standing near her is a person also on stage. Obviously, this person can make out the details of her face better than someone in the first row, and certainly much better than someone in the last row. Perhaps something like the color of her eyes is known to the person on stage but not the audience.

Yet even with this extra knowledge, *from no position in the theatre is anything added to her face.* Her face is what it is, it is only the perspective that varies. Her face is the same but members of the audience contemplate and perceive it differently.

Despite the limitations of this analogy, it helps explain the difference between public and private revelation, and the role of the latter in view of the former.

The word *revelation* literally means "removing the veil." In his infinite goodness and wisdom, God decided to reveal himself to humanity, who without him and without his action, could never know him. Slowly, he began to "remove the veil" which covered his face. Through the patriarchs and prophets of the Old Testament, God gradually began to reveal himself, until Jesus came and the veil was completely removed. In Christ, we could see the fullness of his mystery.

In *Dei Verbum* (*The Word of God*), one of the documents of the Second Vatican Council, we see this description of public revelation:

> In His goodness and wisdom God chose to reveal Himself and to make known to us the hidden purpose of His will by which through Christ, the Word made flesh, man might in the Holy Spirit have access to the Father and come to share in the divine nature. Through this revelation, therefore, the invisible God out of the abundance of His love speaks to men as friends and lives among them, so that He may invite and take them into fellowship with Himself. . . . By this revelation then, the deepest truth about God and the salvation of man shines out for our sake in Christ, who is both the mediator and the fullness of all revelation.[11]

---

[11]   Second Vatican Council, *Dei Verbum* (1965), no. 2.

Jesus is the fulfilment of the revelations hinted at in the Old Testament. According to the Church's teaching, after Jesus, nothing new that is essential for salvation needs to be said about God. Therefore, the Church teaches that all public revelation is contained in the Sacred Scriptures, is interpreted in the light of Holy Tradition, and is taught by the Magisterium of the Church.[12]

However, as the *Catechism of the Catholic Church* puts it, the Church also recognizes that, "throughout the ages, there have been so-called 'private' revelations, some of which have been recognized by the authority of the Church. They do not belong, however, to the deposit of faith. It is not their role to improve or complete Christ's definitive Revelation, but to help live more fully by it in a certain period of history."[13]

Thus, private revelations, such as apparitions approved by the Church, do not add anything new to public revelation but rather underscore some aspects of it that are particularly important for a given time period. In the light of Sacred Scripture, private revelations illuminate some aspects of the mystery of Christ that help people in a particular time or place to live the faith more deeply.

From the moment Fatima was approved by the Church in 1930,[14] it became a private revelation. Our Lady's message

---

[12]   "It is clear, therefore, that sacred tradition, Sacred Scripture and the teaching authority of the Church, in accord with God's most wise design, are so linked and joined together that one cannot stand without the others, and that all together and each in its own way under the action of the one Holy Spirit contribute effectively to the salvation of souls" (*Dei Verbum*, no. 10).

[13]   *Catechism of the Catholic Church*, no. 67.

[14]   Fatima was officially approved by the bishop of Leiria, D. José Alves Correia da Silva, on October 13, 1930.

there does not add anything new to the mystery of Christ. Instead, her words illuminate some aspects of the faith that are especially important for our time. In terms of the analogy of the beautiful woman on stage, the message of Fatima does not change the look of her face, it simply brings us from that back row up onto the stage so that we can better see what has been revealed by the veil's removal.

What Should We Think About Private Revelation?

So what kind of attitude do we take toward private revelation?

If we are honest, we will admit that apparitions are an uncomfortable subject for some, finding them foolish and something only the simple and unsophisticated believe in. Others see apparitions as a challenge to our rationality, which tends to believe only in what we can see, touch, measure, or clearly prove the existence of. Even within the Church, among many schools of theology, apparitions are an inconvenient subject, often only present in the books of Mariology, almost as an appendix.

The official teaching of the Church is clear: private revelations are "reserved for the examination of the Holy See before being published to the people of God" (V Lateran Council, 1516). This means we should be prudent about apparitions not yet approved by the Holy See.

Pope Benedict, then Cardinal Ratzinger, wrote in his theological commentary of the secret of Fatima: "The authority of private revelations is essentially different from that of the definitive public Revelation. The latter demands faith. . . . Faith in God and in his word is different from any other human faith, trust or opinion. The certainty that it is God who is speaking gives me the assurance that I am in touch with truth itself. It gives me a certitude which is beyond verification by any human way of knowing. It is the certitude upon which I build my life and to which I entrust myself in dying."[15]

In that same document, Ratzinger, then the prefect of the Congregation of Faith, quoted Cardinal Prospero Lambertini: "An assent of Catholic faith is not due to revelations approved in this way; it is not even possible. These revelations seek rather an assent of human faith in keeping with the requirements of prudence, which puts them before us as probable and credible to piety."

Although this position articulated by Cardinal Lambertini is commonly accepted, authors such as Father Karl Rahner, one of the most influential twentieth-century theologians, maintain that (approved) private revelation deserves a divine faith. This position is shared by a significant number of current theologians.

In one of Rahner's articles from 1949, titled "Private Revelations: Brief Theological Observations," he addresses from a theological perspective precisely what Church tradition has classified as private revelations, as opposed to public revelations assumed in the biblical cannon. It is within these private revelations that the Fatima event is placed.

In a way, Rahner seems to go against the perspective in which these events are relegated to private character, and to prove his point, he resorts to the Pauline idea that there is no charism in the Church that is not for the good of the

15   Joseph Ratzinger, *The Message of Fatima*, Congregation for the Doctrine of Faith, June 2000.

community (cf. 1 Cor 12–14): "In these 'end of times' there are still some revelations from God. They are not only addressed to private individuals; they are intended for the Church, at least in this sense: that the charism of a member should serve the whole body."[16]

Rahner also disagrees with the idea that a revelation from God could be taken as merely an accessory dimension or something of little significance. "To be satisfied with the statement that the contents of these revelations have a mere accessory relation and close to insignificant relation to the public revelation would raise the question: Can anything coming from God be seen as insignificant?"[17]

Let me repeat him: *Can anything coming from God be seen as insignificant?* I think this question answers itself!

Rahner helps us discern two key ideas: (1) There is, in a way, theological "space" for these revelation events in the life of the Church, and (2) the interest of these events is not restricted to the first witnesses (the "seers") but is of interest to the whole Church.

It's clear Rahner does not see these events as simple advice from heaven. Essentially, he is saying if God speaks through certain instruments, we are obliged to listen, to obey and believe, because it concerns not just those instruments but all of us and the world at large. In this way, for Father Rahner, private revelation holds an indispensable place in the Church.

---

[16]   Karl Rahner, "Les révélations privées. Quelques remarques theologiques", *Revue d'Ascétic et de Mystique*, vol. 25 (1949), p. 506–14.

[17]   Ibid.

So what are we trying to say here with all this "theological" talk?

It is true that the authority of the private revelation is essentially different from the single public revelation. But private revelation supports this faith and it reveals itself as credible because it *appeals* to the single public revelation. In other words, private revelation is built upon the foundation of public revelation. The best attitude to take is one of active discernment, prudent openness, and a wise acceptance and trust in Holy Mother Church.

But let us leave behind the theological talk and discuss something else: the fruit of private revelation. Could the effects we see as a result of certain private revelations not prove their significance and worth?

Since 1830, when Our Lady appeared to Catherine Labouré at a Chapel on Rue du Bac in Paris, more than two hundred apparitions have been reported.[18] Of these, sixteen have been approved by the Holy See.

---

[18]   In reality, since 1830 up until now, 210 miraculous apparitions or events have been registered, of which only 16 have been recognized: Rue du Bac, Paris, 1830, to Saint Catherine Labouré; Rome, 1842, to Alphonse Ratisbonne; La Salette, 1846, to Maximin and Melanie; Rimini, 1850, the image of Mater Misericordiae which was recorded as having Our Lady's eyes move; Taggia (Imperia) 1855, the image of Mary moves her eyes several times; Lourdes, 1858, to Bernadette Soubirous (18 apparitions); Pointmain, 1871, to Eugene Barbedette and other children; Gietrzwald (Poland), 1877, 2 boys and other people; Quito (Equador), 1906, the image of the Sorrowful Virgen moves her eyes over 20 times; Fatima, 1917, Francisco, Jacinta e Lucia, 6 apparitions; Beauraing, 1932, 5 children, 33 apparitions; Banneux, 1933 to Mariette Beco (8 apparitions); Syracuse, 1953, weeping for 4 days, from a plaster plaque of the Immaculate Heart of Mary; Zeitoun (Egypt), 1968,

We can see how significant these apparitions have been by their fruits and by the impact they have in the Church and in society at large. The message Our Lady delivered at Fatima certainly fits into this category, but so do many others.

It is no exaggeration to say that Our Lady's apparitions to Bernadette Soubirous at Lourdes and the shrine established there as a result of those apparitions has changed the lives of the millions who flock there each year. Even though the apparitions of Our Lady of Guadalupe took place in 1531, there is no question that her appearance has had a lasting effect on the lives of millions throughout South, Central, and North America. And of course, the visions of Fatima have created a lasting legacy, as we will see throughout this book.

Many of the places Our Lady has appeared have become places of pilgrimage. Many people have received cures of body or soul in those places; many more have had their lives changed because of these apparitions, with countless conversions being attributed to them. Saints have made pilgrimages to these places and had their vocations or charisms affected by the messages of Our Lady. And the hierarchy of the Church has also been touched by Our Lady's appearances and the urgent messages that she has conveyed on behalf of her Son. Even the most cynical skeptic would be hard pressed to deny all this.

---

the image of the Mother of Light appears on the cupola of the Coptic Church; Akita (Japan), 1973, an image cries more than 101 times; Kibeho (Ruwanda), 1981–1989, Mary appears to 5 students and a nun.

So no, apparitions are not required belief to be a member of the Church, and they should not be compared to public revelation. But they are nonetheless a gift, most especially to the faithful. Pope Francis once said, "If you want to know who Mary is, ask theologians. If you want to know how to love her, you have to ask the people."[19] For many centuries, the people's love for Our Lady has been sweetened through apparitions, and in return, we feel her love through them as well.

Believers vs. People of Faith

Speaking about the increase of faith that the Church's sanctioned apparitions give to the faithful brings to mind a personal experience that illuminates the difference between those who believe and those who have faith. This story illustrates what faith truly is and ultimately helps to explain why Pope Benedict XVI called Fatima a school of faith.

As mentioned previously, some years ago, before becoming vice postulator of the cause of the shepherd children, I was mistress of novices. Our spiritual director, who was also our confessor, had died and we needed to find a new one. Of course, this person also had to be a good and holy director and confessor!

Somebody advised me to go to confession with a certain priest whom we were considering. I told him my sins and difficulties, and after listening to me carefully, he said, "Sister, do you know what your problem is?"

---

[19]   Interview given to the *Civiltà Cattolica* in August/September 2013 issue.

I was so happy that someone was finally going to tell me my problem. With my medical background, I immediately assumed, "He's going to give me a diagnosis, a prognosis, and then a treatment." I thought, "This is great! He'll give me the whole scoop and then I'll be well on my way to making swift spiritual progress!"

Instead, he said gravely, "Your problem, Sister, is that you have no faith!"

I could not believe my ears. My mind raced, and I must admit, some not so holy thoughts crossed my mind. I thought, "How dare you say that to *me*, a superior and mistress of novices!"

Thankfully, he went on to explain what he meant, and it became one of my important lessons about the spiritual life and about Fatima.

He began to talk to me about the Samaritan woman and the conversation she had with Jesus by the well. When Jesus first approached her, her attitude at first was one of arrogance: "How is it that you, a Jew, ask a drink of me, a woman of Samaria?" (Jn 4:9). But then slowly, as the conversation proceeds, she changes her tone. She calls Jesus "Sir" and then "Prophet," and then finally recognizes him as "the Messiah" and "Christ."

The Gospel of John later explains how the Samaritan woman went back to Samaria and urged the Samaritan people, "Come, see a man who told me all that I ever did," and even asked, "Can this be the Christ?" (Jn 4:29).

John then recalls how the Samaritan people, believing in the words of the woman, invited Jesus to stay with them. Jesus stayed for two days, and in the end, the Samaritan people told the woman: "It is no longer because of your words that we believe, for we have heard for ourselves, and we know that this is indeed the Savior of the world" (Jn 4:42).

My spiritual director kept going: "Angela, the Samaritan people at first believed in Jesus based on the words of the woman. They were believers. They believed because someone spoke to them about Jesus. But then they came to believe in Jesus because they had a personal experience with him. They were no longer believers but people of faith."

At first, these two things—believers and people of faith—may seem like the same thing. But they are not. And slowly I began to understand the difference.

It is one thing to have a relationship with Jesus based on the words of others. But it is an entirely different thing to have a personal relationship with Jesus based on our experience of him. The first is good in the beginning; the second is better as we progress in our spiritual journey.

I took this new knowledge and began to consider people who abandon the Church at the first moment of scandal. It is probably because their faith was rooted only upon the faith of others. They had not experienced Jesus for themselves.

Or consider our own personal sufferings. What is our first reaction when an unexpected cross comes into our lives? Does our faith waiver because it was founded upon the faith of others, or is it rooted in Jesus himself?

I have experienced some of this in my life: when in the presence of an unexpected sorrow, my only word to God was a wounded question: Where were you? When in moments of crisis we step away from God, that probably means we were only believers, not people of faith.

My spiritual director, who knew Fatima very well, told me that the primary grace of Fatima is to present us all the conditions necessary to encounter Jesus personally, to have this experience with God, and do so through the person who knows him best: Our Lady.

Inside the Light

To help show how Our Lady and her message at Fatima can bring us into relationship with God, let's look carefully at what Lucia wrote about the first apparition on May 13, 1917.

The last question Our Lady asked them that day was, "Are you willing to offer yourselves to God and bear all the sufferings he wills to send you, as an act of reparation for the sins by which he is offended, and of supplication for the conversion of sinners?"

Lucia replied for all of them, "Yes, we are willing!"

"Then you are going to have much to suffer," she said, "but the grace of God will be your comfort."

Lucia goes on to tell us:

> As she pronounced these last words, Our Lady opened her hands for the first time, communicating to us a light so intense that, as it streamed from her hands, its rays penetrated our hearts and the innermost depths of our souls, making us see ourselves in God, Who was that light, more clearly than we see ourselves in the best of mirrors. Then, moved by an interior impulse

that was also communicated to us, we fell on our
knees, repeating in our hearts: "O most Holy Trinity,
I adore You! My God, my God, I love you in the most
Blessed Sacrament."[20]

The children saw themselves in that immense light, which
was God. Our Lady was giving them the light that was God.
Be not mistaken: Our Lady has no light of her own. The
light of Our Lady is Jesus!

Through this light, she provided them the possibility to
see themselves in God, to see themselves *inside the light*.
After that day, everything was different for the shepherd
children. It was one of the most important moments of the
apparitions when they were able to experience Jesus—his
light—through the hands of Our Lady.

My friends, this is the aim of our spiritual life, to see ourselves in God. To see ourselves as God sees us. Then we will
be able to realize, despite all our sins, vulnerabilities, and
past mistakes, how much we are loved. Our Lady of Fatima
offers us this invitation to take us inside the light.

God knows the fast rhythm of our lives. He knows how
demanding our schedules are, the number of responsibilities
and challenges that fragment our daily lives, taking away our
peace and harmony. This is the nature of our modern lives.
And God knows it even better than we do.

Fatima is a gift uniquely given to us in these challeng-
ing times. It gives us the possibility of "the experience of
God" through the hands of Our Lady, who teaches us how
to encounter him in her very own school of faith. She urges

---

[20]   Lucia dos Santos, *Fatima in Lucia's own words*, p. 176.

us to become, you might say, her "students of faith" so that she can help us to be more than just believers. So she can help make us people of faith.

CHAPTER 3

A Light for the Post-Modern World

A Light Shining in Our Times

"Why did Our Lady have a heart in her hand, spreading out over the world that great light which is God?"[21]

Francisco asked his cousin, Lucia, this simple question. Understandably, we might have questions of our own: What is the meaning of the apparitions? What is the right approach to these events? What can each of us expect, personally, for the Church and for the world in light of the events at Fatima?

Francisco's question actually answers ours: spreading the light of God to the world through the heart of Mary. That is why Fatima radiated a light that shown in the darkness of the early twentieth century and why that light shines into our times as well. How can we enter into this mystery of light and better understand its importance for our lives, for the Church, and for the world?

---

21   Lucia dos Santos, *Fatima in Lucia's own words* (Fátima: Fundação Francisco e Jacinta Marto, 2018), p. 145.

Capturing the Whole Picture

The first time I came to the United States was a trip to Maryland in 1998. I'll never forget the kind welcome and deep interest I encountered about Fatima. I am happy to say that I learned so much in the process of trying to answer all the questions and challenges that American audiences presented to me.

Recent trips to America and other places have helped me notice a profound change in how this miraculous event is considered. Until perhaps as late as the turn of the millennium, Fatima seemed to be just for the uneducated or for poor old women who had nothing else to do but pray the Rosary.

Along these same lines, my talks at first mostly described just the apparitions and presented the "list" of what Our Lady asked us to do (or not do). While these things are obviously important, I found myself unsatisfied. I thought that there had to be more to it than this. I didn't feel we were capturing the whole picture.

It turned out, I was right, but for several years, I did not have the theological "instruments" to do my job well. I did not yet have the hermeneutic principles to see Fatima as a spiritual path in the discipleship of Christ, as being a member of the Church through the Immaculate Heart of Mary.

Thankfully, that has all changed.

Gradually, some theologians, after personal experiences with Our Lady and the event of Fatima, or simply through an open heart and mind that observed the impact of Fatima, began to look at the message of Fatima with a different perspective. These men and women of loftier intellectual prowess began to discern the theological contents present in the message and wrote many good articles and books that highlighted a deeper meaning that had otherwise gone unnoticed. This helped those of us dedicated to the pastoral and spiritual aspects of Fatima be more precise in our teaching and express all of the richness of the message. In short, it helped us capture the whole picture of Fatima.

A Mystical and Prophetic Testimony

The Spanish priest Eloy Bueno de la Fuente presents in his 2014 book *A Mensagem de Fatima* a method of approach to Fatima that, in my opinion, is one of the most complete and unified. He calls the message of Fatima *a mystical and prophetic testimony.*

What exactly does this mean? Let us answer this in a concise way first before going into more detail.

Fatima is first and foremost a *testimony* because it comes to us from three simple children who experienced Our Lady's presence and heard and acted on what she told them. Another word for testimony is *witness*. Lucia, Jacinta, and Francisco were witnesses to something miraculous, something we experience through their eyes and through their words.

These children's experience was *mystical* because, from beginning to end, Fatima reflects the love of the most Holy Trinity for us and gives us a personal experience of God.

Finally, the children's witness is *prophetic* because it shows us that God is still committed to all his children in history. God is not distant and detached. Instead, he reveals himself to be an all-loving, all-good, all-knowing, all-powerful Father.

When we think of something "prophetic," we often think of something that foretells the future, and it is true that at Fatima, Our Lady predicts what will happen if her requests are not met. But the prophetic witness we encounter in the Bible and in many private revelations also invite us to be active participants in the unfolding of history. The prophets of old did not predict the future; they called the people back to God by warning them of what might happen if they did not change their ways and once more embrace God and his will. Likewise, Our Lady of Fatima warned of dire times but also reminded us of our responsibility to come back to God, to ensure our own story is not one of sadness and destruction.

Now let us unpack these a little more.

Testimony

If Fatima is what it is now—a story that millions have heard and a devotion that so many practice all these years later—it is because Francisco, Jacinta, and Lucia answered Our Lady's call the way they did. It is because they lived a certain way.

As the Italian Bible scholar Father Franco Manzi writes, "In order to deepen the theological-moral message of the prophetic visions of the seers of Fatima, it is not enough to examine the 'visual' and 'auditory' content. It is necessary to consider the whole 'spiritual' experience of the three prophets. . . . [This spiritual experience] belongs essentially to the theological-moral content of the visions of Fatima, the cris-tiforme way of living of the three prophets."[22]

I have my own way of saying this. Imagine if, for some reason, the texts of the Angel of Peace and Mary disappeared from the world and all that was left was the biographies of the children, before and after the apparitions. Even if this were the case, we could still see the core of the Fatima message by simply looking at the witness of the children.

Consider it this way: Imagine if all the Bibles and texts about the life of Christ were to disappear from the face of the earth and all that was left to witness to him were our own lives, our words and our deeds. Would non-believers receive the essential message of Christianity simply looking at our way of living and being? A young man once pointed out to me that most non-believers will never pick up a Bible, so, he said, "we are the only Bible they will ever read."

For all of us, the message of Christianity may not be so clear by our way of living. But for these three special children, it is very clear. We see Christ when we look at them. This is something that gets lost in the Fatima story. People tend to focus on the visions of Our Lady or on the secret or on the Miracle of the Sun. We will talk about these things soon enough. But the lives of the children are of just as much importance, and so we will also soon go into greater detail about them. Because they lived a certain way—because of their testimony—we are able to understand the meaning of Fatima all the better.

---

22   Franco Manzi, *Fatima Profezia e Teologia. Lo Sguardo di tre bambini sui Risorti* (Edizioni San Paulo, Milano, 2017), p. 260–261.

Mystical

So what is the mystical nature of Fatima, this "experience of God?" From the very beginning to the end, this story reflects the love of the most Holy Trinity towards all of us. Fatima is an announcement of God's love and mercy towards us.

Some of the Angel of Peace's first words to the children were, "The Hearts of Jesus and Mary have designs of mercy on you."[23] This statement of mercy came in 1916, during the horrors of World War I. In the apparition at Tui many years later in 1929, the last word of the message of Fatima was "mercy." Lucia describes this last apparition, writing, "Under the left arm of the Cross, large letters, as if of crystal clear water which ran down upon the altar, formed these words: Grace and Mercy."[24]

Clearly, Fatima is all about mercy. In other words, Fatima provides an experience of God's love. The first step, the initiative, belongs to God, and so he sent his mother to us. But it is up to us to return this love. As noted earlier, when the Virgin Mary appeared to the children, she asked, "Are you willing to offer yourselves to God?" This is essentially her asking if they are ready to love God, which means to offer themselves to God in order to be testimonies of his compassionate heart, even when that means making difficult sacrifices.

Interestingly, the apparition only goes on *after* Lucia answers for them, "Yes, we are willing!"[25] It is at that point that Our Lady opened her hands for the first time,

---

[23] Lúcia dos Santos, *Fatima in Lucia's own words*, 171.
[24] Ibid., p. 197.
[25] Ibid., p. 175.

communicating a light so intense that it penetrated their hearts and the innermost depths of their souls, making them see themselves in God, who is that light. It is with their yes, then, which in so many ways resembles the *fiat* of the Virgin Mother, that it all begins! This was the beginning of the message of Fatima to the shepherd children: a real and live encounter with the Most Holy Trinity through the hands of the Mother of God.

Whoever wishes to enter into the experience of this message has to be willing to say yes to God in the same way these children (and Mary) did. Only then can God freely carry out his plan of love for us. Our Lady came to Fatima to teach us to have this openness of heart. She wants to create the perfect conditions for our personal encounter with Jesus, an encounter which will transform our lives and allow us to live the virtues of faith, hope, and love.

Our Lady asks us, as she asked them, "Are you willing to offer yourself to God?" The children answered yes. How will you respond? Will you offer yourself?

If we say yes to this fundamental question, the shepherd children's experience will become our experience. We will see ourselves in the light of God; we will see ourselves as God see us, and that vision and God's love will transfigure us. It is no exaggeration to say that this is the aim of our spiritual lives.

Perhaps an analogy may shed some light on the spiritual potential that God is waiting to unlock in all of us. In *La Clairvoyance*, a painting by Rene Magritte, a painter sits before his canvas looking at an egg on a nearby table. But on his canvas, he has not painted the egg but a graceful bird about to take flight. In other words, the painting depicts the *potential* of the egg.

This offers an extraordinary metaphor for our discussion on sanctity and seeing ourselves as God sees us. When we look in the mirror, we do not see a bird in glorious flight but an egg. Yet God, the True Painter, sees the bird about to take flight. He sees our potential, if we would only say yes to him and allow his grace hatch us.

Prophetic

"The mystical experience," says de la Fuente, "contains an enormous prophetic potential: precisely from the experience of love, we can capture all the intensity of what an absence of Love means."[26]

The Spanish author rightly argues that since we know love, we can understand what a lack of love causes, and in this way, he helps us make the transition from the mystical to the prophetic dimension of Fatima.

After World War II and the horrors of the Holocaust, many philosophers and theologians asked where God was when these events happened. At the gates of Auschwitz, then Pope Benedict said:

> To speak in this place of horror, in this place where unprecedented mass crimes were committed against God and man, is almost impossible—and it is particularly difficult and troubling for a Christian, for a pope from Germany. In a place like this, words fail; in the end, there can only be a dreaded silence—a silence

---

[26]   Eloy Bueno de la Fuente, *A Mensagem de Fatima*, p. 197.

> which is itself a heartfelt cry to God: Why, Lord, did
> you remain silent? How could you tolerate all this? . . .
> Constantly the question comes up: Where was God in
> those days? Why was he silent? How could he permit
> this endless slaughter, this triumph of evil?[27]

The Holocaust caused millions to ask where a good God could possibly have been during those horrific times. This is a question all of us ask in our personal lives when we face difficulties and tragedies. As I write this, we are living through the pandemic of the Coronavirus, a plight that is causing much despair. Many people have wondered what God might be doing by allowing such human suffering.

But as a prophetic message, Our Lady's words at Fatima show that God has not forgotten us and that he is still committed to us, individually and globally. Fatima offers a guarantee that God is not far away.

When we hear about prophetic messages, most of us usually think of the Old Testament. But again, prophets are not simply predictors of future events that are guaranteed to take place. They are also witnesses to the truth. Often, they speak in warnings, as the prophets of the Old Testament did, telling the Israelites what would befall them if they did not turn back to God.

And so it is with Fatima. Our Lady's words are a witness to the truth; they draw our attention to the painful events that can occur if we do not convert and return to the God who loves us.

---

[27]   Pope Benedict made these remarks on May 28, 2006.

All the prophetic revelations that we receive—whether in the Old Testament, the New Testament, or in apparitions like those at Fatima—focus on humanity's free will. The whole point of God's communications with us and the warnings that he often gives us is to highlight the fact that we can choose good or evil. The Bible is full of stories that describe the unwanted consequences that can arise when we misuse the gift of our freedom.

At Fatima, Our Lady revealed to the shepherd children many such unfortunate, even tragic, consequences that would occur to the world if people did not turn back to God. She predicted the evils of Communism, of World War II, and the suffering of the Church. Still worse, with the vision of hell, she showed the children the consequences of choosing evil in eternity.

As Mary made clear, without God, there can be no joy and no lasting peace. Her words explain why Pope Benedict describes Fatima as "the most prophetic of the modern apparitions."[28]

Of course, there have been many mystical apparitions, including other Marian apparitions, that contained prophetic-like messages. So why is Fatima different? Why would a man like Benedict say this about Fatima?

Well, for one, approximately seventy thousand people, including many non-believers, witnessed the miracle of the sun, predicted months in advance by the children. No other apparition had such an abundance of witnesses, and this should tell us something about the importance of God's intentions.

---

[28]   Benedict XVI, Aparecida – Brazil, May 13, 2007.

Furthermore, as we will continue to see, almost all the dogmas of the Church are present in the message of Fatima. This theological richness is denser in Fatima than in other apparitions.

Finally, although some may dispute this claim, no other apparition, Marian or otherwise, has had a greater impact on the world, with far-reaching and dramatic geopolitical consequences. While other apparitions might ask for a chapel to be built or a medal to be made, Fatima concerned *the salvation of the whole world.*

The Adoration of Self

We have said much about Fatima, but how is it a "light for the post-modern world," as this chapter indicates? Is it fair to still talk about this apparition a century later as we live in this post-modern world?

Since the Middle Ages, the world has progressively witnessed a change from *theocentrism,* with God being the source and center for understanding the human being and the cosmos, to *anthropocentrism*, which regards man as the center of existence. Gradually, with the Enlightenment and the assertion of reason's preeminence over everything else, modern culture determined that God is no longer necessary or needed for man to understand himself. Through the "masters of suspicion"[29] (Marx, Nietzsche, Freud), we transitioned from a reliance on God to the supremacy of pure reason.

---

[29]   An expression coined by Paul Ricouer.

If, in the eighteenth and nineteenth centuries, the West moved from a focus on God to one on man, in the twentieth-century, that focus shifted again from Man to the Self. It appears that we sacrificed God on the altar of Reason so that we could eventually sacrifice Reason on the altar of Self. The post-modern superhero had to surpass reason and make self-will the only master of truth. In place of a transcendental horizon, we are left with the fragmented remains of self-will.

As the theologian David Bentley Hart puts it, "We live in an age whose highest moral value . . . [is] determined, by overwhelming consensus, to be absolute liberty of personal volition, the power we each have to choose what we believe, want, need or should possess."[30]

Full of himself, the post-modern superman lives to serve the Self at all costs. As a result, he lives an isolated, frag-mented existence, addicted to immediate satisfaction; or perhaps, *the goal of immediate satisfaction,* since he can never actually possess that which he seeks. Moreover, even if he were to achieve his spurious goals, they would not fill his inner void or make him happy. Consequently, because he recognizes that he cannot fully direct what happens to him, he harbors a powerful fear of existence. Since the "core" of such a person is only his wishes and desires, he also cannot escape his fundamental emptiness. Obviously, such a situation is devastating not only to the individual but also to society. As deficient as Reason was as an absolute, at least it was something outside the Self to appeal and measure one's

---

[30]   David Bentley Hart, *Atheist Delusions: The Christian Revolution and its Fashionables Enemies* (Yale University Press: New Haven & London 2009), p. 21–22.

self to. As the sad chronicle of the latter half of the nineteenth century and the entire twentieth century made clear,
when man clings to the Self, he is left only with the ashes of
nihilism.

A world that, with Nietzsche, celebrated "God's death,"
could no longer find reasons to hope, and that is why
Our Lady's message at Fatima was so important when she
appeared, and has become more important with each pass-
ing year. Her message is the answer to the challenges of a
post-modern society, not as a statement of hope, but of
Hope incarnate.

Fatima rejects the temptation to adore and serve the Self
by calling attention to the centrality of God in our lives and
in our history. Fortunately, Our Lady demonstrates that the
solution to the modern spiritual problem is indeed adoration, but of God, not the Self, which never brings happiness.

Fatima's antidote to suffering and the fear of existence is
trust in God and love for the Hearts of Jesus and Mary, who
listen to our prayers and love us with a great and tender
mercy.

To fight our dread of loneliness and isolation, Fatima
invites us to enter into the Immaculate Heart of Mary, our
refuge and way to God, through the Rosary and consecration.

Finally, to heal the wounds of indifference and apathy,
Fatima leads us to solidarity in the good, offering as relief
through reparation and compassion for the suffering of the
world and the Church.

For all these reasons and more, Fatima is a sign of hope to
our world. Our Lady's message is perfectly tailored to heal

our wounds and give us back the light, which, when we are immersed in ourselves, we can no longer find.

The School of Our Lady

On his third trip to Fatima, on May 13, 2000, in his homily for the Beatification Mass of Francisco and Jacinta, John Paul II spoke movingly of the "school" of Our Lady. He told the children in Cova da Iria:

> Ask your parents and teachers to enroll you in the "school" of Our Lady, so that she can teach you to be like the little shepherds, who tried to do whatever she asked them. I tell you that "one makes more progress in a short time of submission and dependence on Mary than during entire years of personal initiatives, relying on oneself alone" (St Louis de Montfort, *The True Devotion to the Blessed Virgin Mary*, n. 155). This was how the little shepherds became saints so quickly. Devoting themselves with total generosity to the direction of such a good Teacher, Jacinta and Francisco soon reached the heights of perfection.[31]

The message of Fatima is a School of Holiness, where the teacher is the Mother of God; the "Teacher of our spiritual life,"[32] as Benedict XVI calls her. Put simply, this is the message of Fatima: a school of faith where the Mother of God teaches God's children to know Jesus Christ.

---

[31]   Pope John Paul II, Homily of Beatification of Blessed Francisco and Jacinta, May 13, 2000, Fatima.

[32]   *Angelus*, 4.03.07.

The world in our time urgently needs graduates of this school, who, like the shepherd children trusting in Our Lady, become "friendly lights"[33] shining on humanity.

---

[33] Pope John Paul II, Homily of Beatification of Blessed Francisco and Jacinta, May 13, 2000, Fatima.

Chapter 4

Fatima, the Trinity, and the Eucharist

Inside the Light

"We stopped, astounded, before the apparition. We were so close, that we were inside the light which surrounded her, or rather, which radiated from her."[34]

This was how Lucia described the first apparition on May 13, 1917, as being "inside the light" that Our Lady radiated.

Fatima is a mystery of light, a light that suffused the shepherd children and covered them like a protective mantle. Pope Francis made this point when he visited Fatima to canonize Francisco and Jacinta and to celebrate the centenary of the apparitions: "According to the belief and experience of many pilgrims, if not of all, Fatima is more than anything this mantle of light that protects us, here as in almost no other place on earth."[35]

---

[34] Lucia de Jesus, *Fatima in Lucia's own words*, vol. 1, 22nd ed. (Fatima: Fundação Francisco e Jacinta Marto, 2018), p. 174.

[35] Pope Francis, May 13, 2017, Homily of the mass of canonization of Sts Francisco and Jacinta, Fatima.

Sister Lucia tells us that for Francisco, "what made the most powerful impression on him and what wholly absorbed him, was God, the Most Holy Trinity, perceived in that light which penetrated our inmost souls. Afterwards, he said: 'We were on fire in that light which is God, and yet we were not burnt! What is God? . . . We could never put it into words. Yes, that is something indeed which we could never express!'"[36]

When people think of Fatima, they do not usually think primarily of the Trinity or the Eucharist. Typically, they think of Mary, or the children, or the miracle of the sun. But now, guided by the Angel of Peace and by Our Lady, and inspired by the example set by the three shepherd children, we are going to enter into the mystery of the Most Holy Trinity, as well as the Eucharist in light of the paschal mystery, present in the message of Fatima, fully conscious, as Francisco was, that it "can never be put into words."

An Experience of God

The message of Fatima took place over thirteen years of apparitions which can be broken down into three cycles:

1. The three apparitions of the angel in 1916 (spring, summer, and autumn)
2. The six apparitions of Our Lady in 1917 at the Cova da Iria (what most think of when they think of Fatima)
3. Two apparitions that involved only Sister Lucia in Spain—Pontevedra and Tui—in 1925 and 1929

---

[36]   Lucia de Jesus, *Fatima in Lucia's own words*, p. 147.

We can see the presence of the Trinity, as well as the Eucharist, in the following apparitions:

- First apparition of the angel – Spring 1916
- Second apparition of the angel – Summer 1916 (although we will not discuss this one in this chapter)
- Third apparition of the angel – Autumn 1916
- First apparition of Our Lady – May 13, 1917
- Second apparition of Our Lady – June 13, 1917
- The apparition of the Most Holy Trinity and Our Lady in the chapel at Tui – June 13, 1929

As this simple summary indicates, from the beginning to the end, the theological horizon of Fatima is painted by the Most Holy Trinity and by Christ present in the Eucharist. This may come as a surprise to some who think Fatima is all about Mary. Of course she is present and is the most important instrument that God used to present this message, but above all, Fatima at its core is all about God and what he wants from us.

Interestingly, however, Our Lady does not teach a dogmatic class about the Trinity or the sacraments, nor does the angel. What they offer is a *personal experience* of God and of the Trinity.

This experience and knowledge of God is transmitted through the apparitions in forms of prayer, all of which are directed not to Mary but to God, Christ, or the Most Holy Trinity, and through the intimate effects of the understanding and experience of the visionaries themselves.

The Prayers of Fatima

There are five new prayers that Fatima gifted to the Church. The first prayer was taught by the angel:

> My God, I believe, I adore, I hope and I love You! I ask pardon of You for those who do not believe, do not adore, do not hope and do not love You.

The second prayer was also taught by the angel:

> Most Holy Trinity, Father, Son and Holy Spirit, I adore You profoundly, and I offer You the most precious Body, Blood, Soul and Divinity of Jesus Christ, present in all the tabernacles of the world, in reparation for the outrages, sacrileges and indifference with which He Himself is offended. And, through the infinite merits of His most Sacred Heart, and the Immaculate Heart of Mary, I beg of You the conversion of poor sinners.

Our Lady then taught the children a new prayer to be prayed after each decade of the Rosary:

> Oh my Jesus, forgive us our sins, save us from the fires of hell. Lead all souls to heaven, especially those who are in most need of your mercy.

The fourth prayer was the one that Our Lady taught the children to say many times, especially to offer their sacrifices:

> Oh my Jesus, it is for the love of thee, for the conversion of sinners, and in reparation for the sins committed against the Immaculate Heart of Mary.

The fifth prayer is one the shepherd children, inspired by the Holy Spirit, prayed at the end of the first apparition in May:

> Oh most Holy Trinity, I adore you! My God, My God,
> I love you in the most Blessed Sacrament.

Five new prayers, all of them dedicated to God or Jesus. This is clear evidence that God is at the center of the Fatima message. And it couldn't be any other way.

As for the intimate effects and the understanding of the experience by the visionaries themselves, we will discuss them in greater detail later in the book. Nevertheless, the prayers show that Our Lady was not stressing only an intellectual formation, although that is important, but the crucial transformation of our hearts.

Now that we have this overall understanding of how God and Christ permeate the message of Fatima, let us dive deeper into some of the specific moments of the apparitions.

"Do Not Be Afraid!"

The first apparition the children experienced was of the Angel of Peace at Loca do Cabeço in the spring of 1916.

Lucia describes it as follows, beginning with what the angel himself said: "'Do not be afraid! I am the Angel of Peace. Pray with me.' Kneeling on the ground, he bowed down until his forehead touched the ground, and made us repeat these words three times: 'My God, I believe, I adore, I hope and I love You! I ask pardon of You for those who do not believe, do not adore, do not hope and do not love You.'"

Then angel then concluded, "Pray thus. The Hearts of Jesus and Mary are attentive to the voice of your supplications."[37]

The angel's first words are interesting. "Do not be afraid! I am the Angel of Peace. Pray with me." What amazing sentences. Fatima opens with a clear invitation not to be afraid!

When we look at society, marked by the threat of terrorism, natural disasters, pandemics, and economic uncertainty, when we look at our families and the challenges we face with health and education, and when we consider our own lives and the loneliness, addiction, and weakness so many face, how can we be anything other than afraid? How is it possible to live without fear?

The answer is in the prayer that the angel taught: "My God, I believe, I adore, I hope and I love You, I ask pardon of You for those who do not believe, do not adore, do not hope and do not love You."

It is impossible to mine all the depths of this prayer, but let us try.

Faith, Hope, and Charity

The first thing that we notice about the angel's words is that the three theological virtues of faith, hope, and charity are at the heart of his prayer. These virtues are given to us from God in the moment of our baptism and serve as the roots of our spiritual life. So from the very beginning, the message of Fatima underlines the sacrament of Baptism, that sacrament which makes us children of God.

---

37   Lucia de Jesus, *Fatima in Lucia's own words*, p. 171.

Before Christ's public life, after his baptism in the Jordan, he heard the voice of his Father: "This is my beloved Son" (Mt 3:17). Then again, shortly before his passion, at the Transfiguration, he heard these words again (see Mt 17:5). In two of the most decisive moments in his life, Jesus heard that he was the beloved Son.

This is why, in moments when he felt alone and misunderstood, even by his closest followers, Jesus was not without hope. In fact, many times Jesus was talking about his death and the apostles were more concerned about who his favorite was (Lk 22:24) or who was the greatest among them (Lk 9:46). Still more, all but one (John) abandoned him while he was on the cross. Even feeling the abandonment of God ("My God, my God, why have you forsaken me?" Mt 27:46), he still recognized God as his Father, intimately uniting himself to all who experience the despair of a life without God, saying, "Father, into your hands I commit my spirit" (Lk 23:46). His confidence in God rose above his suffering.

We are called to this same confidence, my brothers and sisters. If we know we are beloved children of God, we should be able to live a life free of fear. God will not abandon us. This is one of the most important things that we learn from Fatima: that no matter what, our Father will not abandon us. That doesn't mean he takes all our crosses away—he did not even take away the cross from his own Son—but the Father was there with him through it all. From the experience of Jesus, we understand that suffering will always be a part of our life but that God suffers with us.

God does not want suffering, but it is a part of our human condition: we grow old, we get sick, we lose those we love, we die. It is also true that sometimes suffering comes as a consequence of our free choices, of mistakes we make and wrong paths we take. But no matter what, by the power of the Incarnation and the paschal mystery, by the mystery of Jesus's passion and death on the cross, we know that God assumed all our sufferings in Jesus. If we look to Jesus and at the way he offered his life in these moments of the Passion, and we try to live out our own sufferings as he did in obedience to the Father and for the salvation of others, we are participating in the history of salvation in a most precious way.

If we live with this perspective, nothing should bring us to despair. We can cry, we can even complain to God. But we do not fall into despair, and we can live a joyful life despite our sufferings. Fatima's strong message is that we have every reason to hope, even when we walk through this "valley of tears."

Lucia herself said that the purpose of Fatima was to help us grow in faith, hope, and charity. When Cardinal Ratzinger wrote *The Message of Fatima* in 2000, he said, "Allow me to add here a personal recollection: in a conversation with me, Sister Lucia said that it appeared ever more clearly to her that the purpose of all the apparitions was to help people to grow more and more in faith, hope and love—everything else was intended to lead to this."[38]

This came in a conversation Cardinal Ratzinger had with her in 1996, and it was one that resonated with both of

---

[38]   Joseph Ratzinger, *The Message of Fatima*, Congregation for the Doctrine of Faith, June 2000.

them, as Lucia wrote about it as well in her personal diary. This baptismal dimension was at the core of the message of Fatima in her mind: "Thus I see the message ever present in the immense Being of God, to be sent to earth on the day and hour predestined by Him in the designs and plans of his infinite Mercy, in the form of yet another appeal for faith, hope and love."[39]

Adoration

Since Fatima, at its core, is about growing in faith, hope, and charity, the virtues tied to our baptism, then we might ask how we grow in these virtues. In the middle of the prayer the angel gave to the children, we find our answer: "I *adore* You." The call to adoration!

There are many ways to increase and practice the virtues in our lives, but first comes adoration. All other ways to grow in virtue flow from adoration. Without adoration, we cannot live as children of God. Without adoration, we cannot recognize that God is God and we are but creatures.

It may seem to be a very simple thing for all of us, who are human and imperfect and who die, to recognize that we are creatures and not the Creator. But, in fact, this has been the quintessential human problem since the Garden of Eden when Adam and Eve wanted, in the words of the serpent, "to be as gods." We make ourselves our own gods, and we allow all kinds of idols to occupy the place that belongs to

---

[39] Lucia de Jesus, *The Message of Fatima: How I see the Message in the Course of Time and in the Light of Events* (Fatima: Carmelo de Coimbra; Secretariado dos Pastorinhos, 2006), p. 12.

God alone. We want to be the protagonists of our lives and of other peoples' lives.

But the key to happiness is that we only gain our lives if we lose them for the sake of others (see Mt 16:25). We are called to make God and other people the protagonist! This is such a difficult lesson that without adoration, we cannot understand it or live it. Adoration helps us understand we are merely instruments in the hands of God. Without adoration, the idolatry of money, power, or any other temptation sets in.

Adoration also gives us a clearer, more accurate image of God. Many of us fear God because we have a misguided image of him. Some of us think of him as a policeman waiting for us to make a mistake so that he can take us to jail or give us a ticket. Others may feel that God is a judge—weighing our credits and demerits—looking for an occasion to punish us. And still for others, God is a distant, indifferent figure who does not care about them.

Jesus came to show us that God is a loving Father. This means he is merciful and close to us. If we adore him, he reveals himself to us. Through our adoration, we come to truly know him as he truly is, as a Father who loves us.

Holy Communion and an Intense Light

Now we move on to the third apparition of the angel, which is by far the densest, concerning the mysteries of the Trinity and the Eucharist. This time, the angel brought the children Holy Communion in a chalice, with the Host above it dripping drops of blood down into the chalice. The angel left the

Host and the chalice suspended in the air, knelt down, and asked the children to repeat three times:

> Most Holy Trinity, Father, Son and Holy Spirit, I adore You profoundly, and I offer You the most precious Body, Blood, Soul and Divinity of Jesus Christ, present in all the tabernacles of the world, in reparation for the outrages, sacrileges and indifference with which He Himself is offended. And, through the infinite merits of His most Sacred Heart, and the Immaculate Heart of Mary, I beg of You the conversion of poor sinners.

The angel then gave the contents of the chalice to Francisco and Jacinta, and to Lucia the Host. The peace and happiness that they felt was great, as their souls were completely concentrated on God.[40] Francisco would say, "I felt that God was within me but I did not know how it was."[41]

They felt this total absorption into God at the end of the first apparition of Our Lady as well when she opened her hands for the first time and communicated an intense light to them.

Light!

This light is in no way an accidental aspect of the Fatima message. In fact, *light* is one of the most frequent words we hear throughout the story of Fatima. Light, in a spiritual context, is a sign of the presence of the risen Lord and is a manifestation of his glory. Our Lady demonstrates and "speaks"

---

[40]   Lucia de Jesus, *Fatima in Lucia's own words*, p. 173.
[41]   Ibid., p. 142.

about a greater light, the *Light* in itself that is God, the one to whom the Blessed Mother always wants to guide us.

Moved by an interior impulse at seeing and feeling this light, the children fell to their knees, repeating in their hearts the prayer, "Oh most Holy Trinity, I adore you, my God, my God I love You in the most Blessed Sacrament."[42] They prayed this prayer in front of Mary, showing us the perfect union she shares with God. Through this, we see her mission of initiating the people of God with the trinitarian experience.[43]

Francisco captured this bond between Mary and the Trinity with a clear simplicity: "These people are so happy just because you told them that Our Lady wants the Rosary said, and that you are to learn to read! How would they feel if they only knew what she showed to us in God, in her Immaculate Heart, in that great light!"[44]

If we only knew what we could see and know about God in the Immaculate Heart of Mary, I think we would never be afraid and would surrender ourselves to the care of our Blessed Mother. Like her, we would become carriers of the light that is Jesus in us. After all, this is our vocation as disciples of Jesus, like we read in Sacred Scripture: "For it is the God who said, 'Let light shine out of darkness,' who has shone in our hearts to give the light of the knowledge of the glory of God in the face of Christ" (2 Cor 4:6) and, as a

---

[42]   Ibid., p. 176.

[43]   Cf. António Marto, *Fatima: uma luz sobre a história do mundo.* In COUTINHO, Vítor (coord.). *Mensagem de Esperança para o mundo: Acontecimento e significado de Fátima.* (Fátima: Santuário de Fátima, 2012), p. 36-38.

[44]   Lucia de Jesus, *Fatima in Lucia's own words*, p. 146.

consequence, we are called to "shine as lights in the world" (Phil 2:15).

At the end of the second apparition in June, 1917, Lucia again tells us about this amazing light: "As Our Lady spoke these last words, ['My Immaculate Heart will be your refuge and the way that will lead you to God'] she opened her hands and for the second time, she communicated to us the rays of that same immense light. We saw ourselves in this light, as it were, immersed in God. Jacinta and Francisco seemed to be in that part of the light which rose towards Heaven, and I in that which was poured out on the earth."[45]

Lucia, later in her life, would say of this moment,

> It was then that the heavenly Messenger, opening her arms with a gesture of maternal protection, enfolded us in the reflection of the intense Light of the Being of God. It was a grace that left a mark on us forever in the sphere of the supernatural. Oh! Had she not been the Refuge of Sinners, the Mother of Mercy, the Help of Christians, what would have brought Her down to us in order to introduce us, Lord, into the Ocean of your Love, of your Power, of your Immense Being, where this burning flame will cause us to live forever, this mystery of love of the Three for me! It is with this love that I am to adore You, thank You, love You, be transformed into the canticle of your eternal praise.[46]

---

[45]   Ibid., p. 177.

[46]   Lucia de Jesus, *The message of Fatima*, p. 44.

Lucia's Vision in Tui and the Angel's Prayer

Now, let us discuss the last cycle of apparitions, detailing what Sister Lucia saw in Tui in June of 1929, when the mystery of the Most Holy Trinity was clearly united to the mystery of the Eucharist.

Many years ago, as I was preparing my first talk about Fatima and the Eucharist, I went to visit Jesus in the Blessed Sacrament. On this particular occasion, I had brought a picture that someone had drawn of the apparition of Tui and placed it before my eyes.

As I began my hour of adoration with the prayers of the angel, kneeling there in front of Jesus in the tabernacle and looking at the painting of Tui, I realized that what Lucia saw in 1929 was what she had been praying since 1916. God allowed me to understand how clearly Fatima, from the beginning to the end, was about the most Holy Trinity and the Eucharist.

This becomes clear if we examine what Lucia actually saw that day.

On June 13, she had asked her superior to do an hour of Eucharistic adoration. She explains, "I had sought and obtained permission from my superiors and confessor to make a Holy Hour from eleven o'clock until midnight, every Thursday to Friday. Being alone one night, I knelt near the altar rails in the middle of the chapel and, prostrate, I prayed the prayers of the Angel. Feeling tired, I then stood up and continued to say the prayers with my arms in the form of a cross. The only light was that of the sanctuary lamp."[47]

---

[47]   Lucia de Jesus, *Fatima in Lucia's own words*, p. 197.

Notice the darkness in the chapel, and how vividly Lucia recalls that the only light came from the sanctuary lamp. This can be a metaphor for our spiritual life at times, when everything looks dark. If we don't pay attention to the light that comes from the tabernacle—from Jesus—we will be in total darkness.

Lucia then saw something which draws remarkable comparisons to the prayer of the angel. The following table makes these comparisons clear:

The prayer of the Angel (1916)	Vision of Tui (1929)
Most Holy Trinity, Father, Son and Holy Spirit, I adore you profoundly . . .	Suddenly the whole chapel was illumined by a supernatural light, and above the altar appeared a cross of light, reaching to the ceiling. In a brighter light on the upper part of the cross, could be seen the face of a man and his body as far as the waist, upon his breast was a dove also of light and nailed to the cross was the body of another man.

. . . and I offer you the most precious Body, Blood, Soul and Divinity of Jesus Christ . . .	A little below the waist, I could see a chalice and a large host suspended in the air, on to which drops of blood were falling from the face of Jesus Crucified and from the wound in His side. These drops ran down on to the host and fell into the chalice.
. . . present in all the tabernacles in the world . . .	Lucia was in an hour of Eucharistic adoration, before the tabernacle in her chapel.
. . . and through the infinite merits of his most Sacred Heart and the Immaculate Heart of Mary . . .	Beneath the right arm of the cross was Our Lady and in her hand was her Immaculate Heart (it was Our Lady of Fatima, with her Immaculate Heart in her left hand, without swords or roses, but with a crown of thorns and flames).
. . . I beg of you the conversion of poor sinners.[48]	Under the left arm of the cross, large letters, as if of crystal clear water which ran down upon the altar, formed these words: 'Grace and Mercy.'[49]

---

[48]   Ibid., p. 172.
[49]   Ibid., p. 197–98.

In just a glimpse, Lucia saw the most important mysteries of our faith: the mystery of the Most Holy Trinity, the incarnation of Christ, the Second Person of the Trinity, the redemptive sacrifice of Christ in union with the Eucharist, and, finally, the presence and the unique role of Mary in the history of salvation. She shows us that she is still the "woman" by the cross, as John states in chapter 19 of his Gospel. There, she intercedes for us. In union with the prayer of Jesus, she is pleading to the Father, "I beg you for the conversion of poor sinners." She is asking for "grace and mercy." It's an announcement to our world that God is giving us all the grace and all the mercy we need.

CHAPTER 5

The Eucharist: Believed, Celebrated, and Lived

Sacramentum Caritatis

Following our reflections on the Trinitarian and Eucharistic elements of the Fatima message, it would do us well to discuss how we put this knowledge to good use. To help us do this, we can turn to Benedict XVI and his post-synodal Apostolic Exhortation *Sacramentum Caritatis (The Sacrament of Charity)*.[50]

Benedict divides this exhortation on the Eucharist into three parts:

1. The Eucharist, a mystery to be *believed*.
   What do we believe when we say that we believe in the Eucharist?
2. The Eucharist, a mystery to be *celebrated*.
   What do we celebrate, and how can we celebrate the Eucharist?

---

[50]   Benedict XVI, *Sacramentum caritatis*, Post Synodal apostolic exhortation on the Eucharist, Feb. 22, 2007.

3. The Eucharist, a mystery to be *lived*.
   Is the Eucharist just something for me to believe
   and celebrate or does it have something to do with
   my daily life?

Let us look at each of these parts, one at a time.

A Mystery to Be Believed

The Holy Father emphasizes Christ's personal and total gift of himself to each of us in the Eucharist, in which "Jesus does not give us a 'thing', but himself; he offers his own body and pours out his own blood. He thus gives us the totality of his life and reveals the ultimate origin of this love."[51]

At each Mass, Christ gives himself totally to us. The bishop of Fatima, Cardinal Antonio Marto, explains the relationship between the Eucharist and Christ's passion and death (the paschal mystery) when he writes, "In the Eucharist of the Last Supper, the mystery was anticipated; on the Cross it was consummated; in the Resurrection it was eternalized; in our celebration it is actualized, making it present by the presence of the Resurrected One."[52]

The treasures of the Eucharistic mystery are born from the treasures of the pashcal mystery. Jesus gives himself to us not because we are good people, nor because we have enough merits to deserve this, but because he loves us to that extent.

So the Eucharist is not some *thing*, it is *Someone*; it is Jesus, giving himself to me, now, offering me his salvation

---

[51]   Ibid.

[52]   António Marto, *Eucaristia e Beleza de Deus* (Viseu: Fundação Jornal da Beira, 2005), p. 21.

and his own life, his "life in abundance" (Jn 10:10). But this is something we can only come to know through faith; in other words, if we *believe*. We are called to believe in the mystery of the Eucharist, since our senses do not inform us that we are receiving anything other than bread and wine.

Naturally, the Holy Scriptures help us see the truth of Christ's presence in the Eucharist, but the Fatima apparitions help to buttress our belief. The vision given to Sister Lucia at Tui helps us contemplate to what extent the Eucharistic mystery is profoundly united with the paschal and Trinitarian mysteries.

A Mystery to Be Celebrated

In his exhortation, Benedict XVI underlines three elements of the Eucharistic celebration: (1) The Mass – the Eucharistic celebration itself, (2) The Post-communion moment, and (3) Eucharistic Adoration.

In regards to the Mass, Benedict reminds us that the "Eucharistic celebration is the greatest act of adoration of the Church."[53]

The three shepherd children understood this well, frequently taking part in the celebration of Mass not only on Sundays but also attending daily Mass. Once when Lucia told Jacinta she didn't need to go to Mass because she was sick and it was not a Sunday, Jacinta replied, "It doesn't matter. I go for sinners who don't even go on Sundays."[54] And keep in mind they would've had to walk a mile to get there.

---

[53] Benedict XVI, *Sacramentum caritatis*, 66.

[54] Lucia de Jesus, *Fatima in Lucia's own words*, vol. 1, 22nd ed. (Fátima: Fundação Francisco e Jacinta Marto, 2018), p. 126.

Later, when the authorities were sent in to intimidate the children and others in town from visiting the Cova da Iria, and many warned Lucia that she could be killed, she without hesitation left her house to attend Mass in the church near where the guards were stationed.

The seers of Fatima recognized the Holy Mass as a place where they received and embraced the greatest of gift—God himself—and where they in turn offered themselves as a gift, particularly through the suffering they would encounter.

They also saw the Mass as a moment for intercession, as a moment where those in greatest need are remembered, and as a place of Christian commitment for the good of others.

Francisco said to Lucia shortly before he died, "Now listen, you must also ask Our Lord to forgive me my sins."

Lucia responded, "I'll ask that, don't worry. Now, I'm going to Mass, and there I'll pray to the Hidden Jesus for you."[55]

These simple stories reveal to us the importance of the Eucharistic celebration in the lives of the seers. In Lucia's writings in particular, we are able to see how the Eucharist becomes an unavoidable place of encounter with God in the truly decisive moments of her life.

This challenges us to look at our own participation at Mass. We must ask ourselves if this is the anchor of our spiritual lives and if it is something we truly mean to *celebrate*. Are we willing to go to great lengths, like Jacinta, to get to Mass? Or do we neglect our participation and search for excuses to miss? Are we willing to go there, like Lucia, even if it spells danger for us? Do we look to the Eucharist

---

[55] Ibid., p. 164.

as something that important, that we cannot miss a single chance to celebrate it? And while there, do we make a gift of ourselves for others? Do we intercede on behalf of others, of sinners?

These last questions remind us that it is not enough just to be there. We must mentally and spiritually be "on our game" while we sit in the pew. This brings us to the importance Benedict placed on the post-communion moment, after we have just received Our Lord. The pope stated it with clarity: "Furthermore, the precious time of thanksgiving after communion should not be neglected: besides the singing of an appropriate hymn, it can also be most helpful to remain recollected in silence."[56]

In many places, we neglect this moment, be it by distraction or by inappropriate hymns. Sometimes people also leave after communion. Imagine how hurtful it would be to any of us if we invited a guest to come to a meal at our home, and in the middle of the meal, he or she simply got up and left? How impolite and rude that would be! The proper thing would be for us to be together, talking, sharing a little of our lives, keeping each other company.

When we go to Communion, it is as if we have invited Jesus into our home. And how do we act as hosts? Do we leave him alone, act distracted, think about everything but him, or even forget he is with us? Do we fail to thank him for coming and for the gift of his life and his love?

Lucia leaves us a moving witness about how close Jesus is to each of us in the Eucharist.

---

[56]   Benedict XVI, *Sacramentum caritatis*, 50.

One day after Lucia had been to Mass, when she was going past Jacinta's house, Jacinta said to Lucia, "Come over here close to me, for you have Jesus hidden in your heart."[57] This may seem like a childish fancy, but Jacinta's words signal a profound faith in the real presence of Jesus in the Eucharist.

Francisco, after he had received Communion, said something similar just before he died: "Today I am happier than you, because I have the hidden Jesus within my heart."[58] This is a boy who knew he was going to die within the next few hours. How amazing! He was going to die—he knew that— and the source of his happiness was that he had just received Communion. Jacinta and Francisco's witness demonstrates how essential the Eucharist was to their lives.

Finally, in his exhortation, Pope Benedict XVI underlines the key role Eucharistic adoration should play in the life of the faithful:

> In the Eucharist, the Son of God comes to meet us and desires to become one with us; eucharistic adoration is simply the natural consequence of the eucharistic celebration, which is itself the Church's supreme act of adoration. Receiving the Eucharist means adoring him whom we receive. Only in this way do we become one with him, and are given, as it were, a foretaste of the beauty of the heavenly liturgy. The act of adoration outside Mass prolongs and intensifies all that takes place during the liturgical celebration itself. Indeed, only in adoration can a profound and genuine

---

[57] Lucia de Jesus, *Fatima in Lucia's own words*, p. 133.
[58] Ibid., p. 165.

reception mature. And it is precisely this personal encounter with the Lord that then strengthens the social mission contained in the Eucharist, which seeks to break down not only the walls that separate the Lord and ourselves, but also and especially the walls that separate us from one another.[59]

The three seers were keen to be near the "Hidden Jesus," as they called him, taking every opportunity to be in his presence. Jacinta loved to visit the Blessed Sacrament on breaks. Frustrated once by the crowds flocking to them, she lamented not being able to sit in silent adoration: "We are no sooner inside the church than a crowd of people come asking us questions! I wanted so much to be alone for a long time with the Hidden Jesus and talk to him, but they never let us."[60]

Francisco's spirituality was especially marked by this love for the Hidden Jesus. Lucia tells us, "Sometimes on our way to school, as soon as we reached Fatima, he would say to me: 'Listen! You go to school, and I'll stay here in the church, close to the Hidden Jesus. It's not worth my learning to read, as I'll be going to Heaven very soon. On your way home, come here and call me." Lucia continues, "Later, when he fell ill, he often told me, when I called in to see him on my way to school: 'Look! Go to the church and give my love to the Hidden Jesus. What hurts me most is that I cannot go there myself and stay awhile with the Hidden Jesus.'"[61]

---

[59]   Benedict XVI, *Sacramentum caritatis*, 66.
[60]   Lucia de Jesus, *Fatima in Lucia's own words*, p. 55.
[61]   Ibid., p. 157.

Nothing else could fill his heart. To be with the Hidden Jesus was his joy and the whole purpose of his days. Francisco recognized that Jesus is hidden not only because he cannot be outwardly seen in the Eucharist but because he invites us to contemplation, to intimacy, to the endless dialogue in the secret corners of our hearts where we cultivate our friendship with Christ.

When we want to celebrate something, we seek out friends and family. We flock to them, for no one celebrates alone. The union of hearts increases the joy of the occasion. This was how the children viewed Eucharistic adoration, as a celebration of their friendship with Christ.

A Mystery to Be Lived

Once we come to believe in the truth of the Eucharist and know we must celebrate Jesus in the Eucharist, we can begin to live out this mystery.

Pope Benedict explains how our faith in the Eucharist and our lives cannot be separated:

> The Christian faithful need a fuller understanding of the relationship between the Eucharist and their daily lives. Eucharistic spirituality is not just participation in Mass and devotion to the Blessed Sacrament. It embraces the whole of life. This observation is particularly insightful, given our situation today. It must be acknowledged that one of the most serious effects of the secularization just mentioned is that it has relegated the Christian faith to the margins of life as if it were irrelevant to everyday affairs. . . . Today there is

a need to rediscover that Jesus Christ is not just a private conviction or an abstract idea, but a real person, whose becoming part of human history is capable of renewing the life of every man and woman. Hence the Eucharist, as the source and summit of the Church's life and mission, must be translated into spirituality, into a life lived "according to the Spirit" (Rom 8:4ff.; cf. Gal 5:16, 25).[62]

This is where everything gets more complex and difficult, because living a Eucharistic life means to live life as a gift of self, as a donation of self, and this is something that challenges us.

Eucharistic spirituality is not just participating in Mass and devotion to the Blessed Sacrament. It embraces one's whole life. And what is Jesus doing in the first Eucharist and the paschal mystery? He is giving his life to others, even if the others don't want to receive it, or refuse it or ignore it. To be a Eucharistic person is to live life like this, as a gift to others, even if others don't appreciate the gift we offer. Benedict referred to this way of living as "Eucharistic coherence,"[63] uniting our lives to the Eucharist so intimately that we surrender ourselves to God for the good of others.

This way of life is the foundation of the Fatima message, as Our Lady made clear when, at her first apparition, she asked the children, "Do you want to offer yourselves to God?"

We know Lucia responded with a generous yes on behalf of the three children. God initiated their encounter, but that

---

62   Benedict XVI, *Sacramentum caritatis*, 77.
63   Ibid., 83.

encounter is sustained and enriched through the children's response and participation. Their freedom and their desire are also now involved. Once they respond and participate, what happens at Fatima is no longer merely the story of God with them, it also becomes the story of the shepherd children *with* God.

The offering of their lives, their sacrifices which they will make for "poor sinners," is all done against the backdrop of and in union with Jesus's Eucharistic offering of himself. As Lucia explains, this is already clear in the third apparition of the angel: "Then, rising, he once more took the chalice and the host in his hands. He gave the host to me, and to Jacinta and Francisco he gave the contents of the chalice to drink, saying as he did so: 'Take and drink the Body and Blood of Jesus Christ, horribly outraged by ungrateful men. Repair their crimes and console your God.'"[64]

This moment seals the shepherd children's commitment. As one writer of the Fatima story points out, "These children do not limit themselves to take communion from the chalice of Christ and Christ in the Chalice, but they themselves were transformed, through their suffering, . . . into a new chalice, that they themselves drank, not out of despair, but in loving fulfillment of what the Angel and the Lady had asked them: the sacrificial offering on behalf of the good of the salvation of all humanity."[65]

The children were only able to console God (the most striking feature of Francisco's personality) and offer themselves

---

[64] Lucia de Jesus, *Fatima in Lucia's own words*, p. 172.
[65] Américo Pereira, "*A Paz do anjo, paz de Deus*", in Fatima XXI. n.º 5. (Fatima: Santuário de Fátima, 2016), p. 64.

for the good of others (the most striking feature of Jacinta's) because they themselves drank from the chalice of Jesus. They would not have been familiar with Christ's description of himself as the Bread of Life in the sixth chapter of the Gospel of John, but they had personally experienced and drawn strength from the Body and Blood of Our Lord, from the very life of Christ, so as to offer themselves as "the perfect spiritual sacrifice" (cf. Rm 12:1) for others.

Perhaps no story better displays the children's passionate surrender for the good of humanity and their union with Christ than the one Lucia relays about Jacinta's walking through the pastures one day while holding a lamb. When Lucia questions her cousin, asking why Jacinta is amidst the sheep, she replies, "I want to do the same as Our Lord in that holy picture they gave me. He's just like this, right in the middle of them all, and He's holding one of them in His arms."[66]

To do what Our Lord did, to be like Jesus, that was Jacinta's life (as we will see in a later chapter). She wanted to live as a gift to others, even those she did not know. She did this out of love, out of passion, because she was consumed by a fire that inflamed her heart but did not burn her. It was a fire that unsettled her, because she understood that there were "poor sinners" lost and confused "like sheep without a shepherd" (Mk 6:34). She wanted to go to heaven, but she couldn't stand the idea of going to heaven alone or the fact that not everyone would be going there too!

Even at the end of her life, when a terrible wound on her chest caused her great discomfort, she wanted to console the

---

66   Lucia de Jesus, *Fatima in Lucia's own words*, p. 44.

pilgrims who asked her to intercede for them, she wanted to convert more poor sinners, she wanted the Holy Father not to suffer, she wanted to console the Heart of Jesus and the Immaculate Heart of Mary. This open wound on her chest made her an intimate *confidante* of the Crucified, and helped her understand the mystery of surrender present in the Lord's passion.

And because Jacinta wanted "to do as Our Lord," she learned to forget herself in the little things of her everyday life, which were centered on gestures of surrender and denial. In the eyes of the world, these gestures of surrender were insignificant, but they formed her spirit in such a way that when the great and difficult moments of her life came, she was able to configure herself more and more with Jesus's surrender. This is, as Pope Benedict comments, one of the most beautiful secrets of Fatima: "the extraordinary way in which these children surrendered their lives for the good of others, drinking to the end the chalice that Our Lord, in his mercy, allowed them to drink."[67] In this way, they show us what it means to live the mystery of the Eucharist.

Freeing a Small Friend

Francisco and Jacinta belong, undoubtedly, to that group of Christians who, as Benedict XVI teaches, profoundly understand that "Eucharistic spirituality is not only participating in the Mass and devotion to the Blessed Sacrament; but embraces our whole life."[68] Their vocation is a Eucharistic life lived for the good of others.

---

67   May 12, 2010, Fatima address.
68   Benedict XVI, *Sacramentum caritatis*, 77.

A closing story shows how Francisco in particular lived this Eucharistic life. Lucia tells us:

> One day we met a little boy carrying in his hand a small bird that he had caught. Full of compassion, Francisco promised him two coins, if only he would let the bird fly away. The boy readily agreed. But first he wished to see the money in his hand. Francisco ran all the way home from the Carreira pond, which lies a little distance below the Cova da Iria, to fetch the coins, and so let the little prisoner free. Then, as he watched it fly away, he clapped his hands for joy, and said: "Be careful! Don't let yourself be caught again."[69]

You may be saying, "Sister, what on earth does this cute but simple story have to do with living out the mystery of the Eucharist?"

Well, I will tell you.

The beauty of this simple story is that through Francisco's sacrifice, all the other participants in the story gain something. The little friend gets money and the bird gains his freedom. Technically, Francisco is the "loser." He loses his time in going home to get the coins, he loses the coins themselves, and he loses the bird. From an earthly perspective, Francisco wins nothing. But he has the joy of watching the bird, for whom he has sacrificed, fly away.

This story shows Francisco's generous heart, that he can take such joy in freeing a bird at his own expense. Even though he knows the bird can be captured again, and that

---

[69]   Lucia de Jesus, *Fatima in Lucia's own words*, p. 159.

the bird will eventually die, Francisco gives of himself so that bird is able to be true to its very nature and free to fly.

The elements of this story are reminiscent of Jesus's offering himself for us, for our freedom from sin and death. Christ freely accepts the loss of everything, even of his own life, so that we can be fully human, so that we can be fully free to choose God and eternal life.

Like Jesus, Francisco sees that his role is to live life as a gift for others. This is a Eucharistic life. Like Jesus, Francisco joyously embraces his "losses" without even receiving thanks.

Until we get to this point, where we are willing to live a life as a gift to others with no promise of reward or gratitude, we do not live as true children of God. But Fatima helps us grow in that process. That is the good news. And it is *a process*, something that can take the whole of our lives. Learning how to die to self so that others may have a life does not happen overnight.

The Importance of Gratitude

Focusing on the importance of living the mystery of the Eucharist is inseparable from focusing on gratitude. The word *eucharist* means *thanksgiving*. To live a Eucharistic life is to live in constant gratitude to God. Harboring this gratitude helps us in this process of dying to self and making a gift of ourselves, for when we are thankful, we want to act upon that gratitude, we want to repay the blessings that have been bestowed upon us in whatever small way we are able.

Jacinta would often ask the other two, and in the process she asks all of us, "Have you been forgetting to tell Our Lord how much you love him for the graces he has given us?"[70] Like the three children, let us pray many times a day with a genuine Eucharistic attitude of thanksgiving: "My God, I love You, in thanksgiving for the graces which You have granted me."[71]

The Heart of Fatima

John Paul II, the bishop dressed in white, who kept Fatima tenderly in his heart, reminded us that "the Eucharist is the heart of the Church. And where the Eucharistic life thrives, the life of the Church thrives."[72]

The heart of Fatima beats with a Eucharistic rhythm, and it invites the whole Church to synchronize its heart with her beating. How is this possible? Because the heart of Fatima is the Immaculate Heart of Mary! As the Mother of God, she learned the "rhythm of Christ" by living and contemplating all the mysteries of his life, and as the Mother of the Church, she can synchronize our hearts to that beautiful rhythm.

When we contemplate Lucia's great vision at Tui, we are invited to live in union with the Eucharistic mystery, which will allow us to reach the perfection of charity.

Pope Benedict once said, "The Lady who 'came from heaven,' the Teacher who introduced the little seers to a deep knowledge of the love of the Blessed Trinity and led them to savor God himself as the most beautiful reality of human

---

[70]   Ibid., p. 92.
[71]   Ibid., p. 91.
[72]   John Paul II, Speech to the clergy and religious people, September 14, 1980, Siena.

existence. This experience of grace made them fall in love with God in Jesus."[73]

This is what Our Lady wants to do with each one of us: let us experience God as the most beautiful reality of human existence!

---

[73]   Benedict XVI, Homily, May 13, 2010, Fatima.

Chapter 6

The Secret

Understanding the Nature of Prophecy

"Fatima is the most prophetic of the modern apparitions,"[74] said Pope Benedict XVI. But as we mentioned before, a prophet is not a fortune-teller. In the biblical sense, a prophet is a man or woman of faith who grounds their existence in God's Word and who speaks to the faithful on behalf of God. They do not so much predict the future as interpret the signs of the times and call the people back to God, often through warnings of what will happen if they don't return. From this perspective, we will dissect Fatima and the words and actions of the three shepherd children as what you might call "modern day prophets."

To do this, we must understand the double dimension of a prophecy: *denouncing* and *announcing*. This first quality denounces all behaviors and choices that deny God. A prophet speaks out against sin and its consequences, moral decay, and everything that can lead man to death, war,

---

[74]   Benedict XVI, Aparecida, Brasil, May 13, 2007.

and disharmony. But, at the same time, there is also the announcement of salvation, the foundation for our hope.[75]

All this is present throughout the apparitions of Fatima, but more specifically in the secret of Fatima, which was witnessed by the seers on July 13, 1917.

Revealing the Secret

A common misunderstanding of the Fatima secret is that there were three secrets, *when in fact it is a single secret with three parts.* Each of these "parts" were published by the Church at different times, the last on June 26, 2000, though Lucia had written about them much earlier at the behest of the bishop of Leiria, D. José Alves Correia da Silva, in 1941. (When she grew ill and the bishop feared she would die, he had her write down the third part of the secret, but it was only revealed to the public in 2000.)

It has been documented how Lucia struggled to obey the bishop's orders, feeling she did not yet have the permission of heaven. She wrote in her diary:

> If only my strength allowed me to, I wanted to write what the Bishop had ordered me but I cannot explain what was happening to me as my hand shook and I could not form the words. This may have been caused by my impression that I had to write something against the orders of Our Lady, but still by obedience. I attempted several times without getting any results.

---

[75] Leo Scheffczyk, A mensagem de Paz. In COUTINHO, Vítor (coord.). *Mensagem de Esperança para o mundo: Acontecimento e significado de Fátima.* (Fátima: Santuário de Fátima, 2012), p. 289.

Because of this conflict, I wrote the Bishop of Leiria, telling him what was happening to me. His Excellency replied by renewing the order he had already given me, perhaps in more expressive terms, in a letter dated October 16th 1943. After receiving this letter, I wanted to write again, but I still did not succeed.[76]

In this conflicting state, Lucia, on January 3, 1944, went to pray. Let us see how she describes what happened next:

On January 3rd 1944, I knelt beside the bed which sometimes served as a writing table, and again I experienced the same without success. What most impressed me was that at the same moment I could write anything else without difficulty. I then asked Our Lady to let me know if it was the Will of God. I went to the Chapel at 4 p.m. in the afternoon, the hour that I always made a visit to the Blessed Sacrament because I was ordinarily alone. I do not know why, but I liked being alone with Jesus in the Tabernacle.

Then I knelt in the middle, next to the rung of the Communion rail and asked Jesus to make known to me what was His Will. Accustomed as I was to believe that the order of the Superior was the expression of the Will of God, I couldn't believe that this wasn't. Feeling puzzled and half absorbed under the weight of a dark cloud that seemed to hang over me, with my face between my hands, I hoped without knowing how for a response. I then felt a friendly, affectionate

---

[76] Carmel of Coimbra, *A Pathway under the gaze of Mary* (Washington, NJ: World Apostolate of Fatima, 2015), p. 241.

and motherly hand touch me on the shoulder and I looked up and saw the beloved Mother from Heaven. "Do not be afraid, God wanted to prove your obedience, faith and humility. Be at peace and write what they order you, but not what has been given you to understand its meaning. After writing it, place it in an envelope, close it and seal it and write on the outside that this can be opened only in 1960 by the Cardinal Patriarch of Lisbon or by the bishop of Leiria."

I felt my spirit flooded by a mystery of light that is God and in Him I saw and heard: – The tip of the spear as a flame unlatches and touches the axis of the earth, – It shudders: mountains, cities, towns, villages with their inhabitants are buried. The sea, the rivers, and the clouds emerge from their limits, overflowing and bringing with them in a whirlwind houses and people in numbers that are not possible to count. It is the purification of the world because of sin as it plunges. Hatred and ambition cause the destructive war! Then I felt the rapid beating of my heart and in my mind the echo of a gentle voice saying: "In time, one faith, one baptism, one Church, Holy, Catholic, and Apostolic. In eternity, Heaven."

This word Heaven filled my soul with peace and happiness, so that almost without realizing it, I was repeating for a long time: Heaven! Heaven! As soon as the full force of the supernatural passed, I went to write, without difficulty on January 3, 1944 on my knees, resting on the bed that served me as a table.[77]

---

[77]   Ibid., p. 243–44.

As we can see, in this hour of adoration, when Lucia is asking for guidance, she experiences another supernatural event, a mystical experience concerning the suffering of the world. But this has nothing to do with the secret itself. There were no more secrets to reveal here or at other times, as some conspiracy theorists posit. What this vision did was give her the assurance that she was permitted to reveal the third part of the secret. Lucia then did so and found a trustworthy person who could give this information to the bishop of Leiria.

Below is a timeline of what happened from that point onward:

- **12/8/1945** – The bishop of Leiria places the sealed envelope, which he received with the third part of the secret, in another sealed envelope, which he wax-sealed with the episcopal seal, stating that after his death the envelope should be delivered to the cardinal-patriarch of Lisbon.
- **3/1/1957** – The manuscript of the third part of the secret is delivered to the Apostolic Nunciature of Lisbon by Bishop João Pereira Venâncio, auxiliary bishop of Leiria.
- **4/4/1957** – The manuscript of the third part of the secret reaches the Vatican, to be kept in the secret archive of the Holy Office (the current Congregation for the Doctrine of Faith).
- **8/17/1959** – Pierre Paul Philippe, commissioner of the Holy Office, delivers the manuscript with the third part of the secret to Pope John XXIII in Castel Gandolfo and in the presence of his private secretary,

Loris Capovilla. The Holy Father decided that he would reserve the moment of reading for later, to be done when he was in the presence of his confessor.

- **8/21/1959** – John XXIII, accompanied by his confessor, read the manuscript with the third part of the secret. To better understand its content, he calls for a translator of the Curia, Paulo Jose Tavares, future bishop of Macau. After reading the manuscript, Pope John XXIII decides not to reveal the content publicly and instead keeps it on his desk at the Vatican, where it remained until his death.

- **3/27/1965** – Pope Paul VI reads the document written by Lucia and in so doing becomes aware of the third part of the secret. After reading it, he, too, decides not to reveal it.

- **5/13/1981** – Pope John Paul II is shot by a Turkish assassin on the anniversary of the first apparition of Our Lady of Fatima, whom he would later credit for saving his life. In the weeks following, while in recovery, he asks for the manuscript containing the secret to be brought to him so he can read it.

- **7/18/1981** – Responding to the request from John Paul II, Franjo Seper, prefect of the Congregation for the Doctrine of the Faith, delivers the manuscript and the translation in Italian to Eduardo Martinez Somalo, substitute for the secretariat of state, so he could deliver it to the pope.

- **08/11/1981** – Lucia's manuscript is once again sent to the secret archive of the Congregation for the Doctrine of the Faith.

- **5/12/1982–5/15/1982** – John Paul II takes an apostolic trip to Portugal, making himself a pilgrim of the Sanctuary of the Cova da Iria, in thanksgiving to the Virgin of Fatima for the maternal protection on the day of his attack. He meets with Lucia, who says in her diary of their private meeting on May 13 in the Retreat House of Our Lady of Carmel: "We spoke about the secret and we agreed that it would be more prudent to keep it in silence as was done up until now."[78]

- **1985** – A book is released containing a long interview with Cardinal Joseph Ratzinger, prefect of the Congregation for the Doctrine of the Faith, to the journalist Vittorio Messori, in which the cardinal admits having read the manuscript of the third part of the secret. He explains that the content of this manuscript had not yet been revealed due to the fact that the pope believed it would add nothing new "to what a Christian should know by the revelation" and that its content could "expose itself . . . to the dangers of sensationalist use."[79]

- **4/27/2000** – Tarcisio Bertone, as the papal envoy, meets Lucia in the Carmel of Santa Teresa in Coimbra, in order to analyze the manuscript of the

---

[78]   Lucia de Jesus, *Apud Carmelo de Coimbra, A Pathway Under the Gaze of Mary* (Washington, NJ: World Apostolate of Fatima, 015), p. 376.

[79]   Joseph Ratzinger, *Vittorio Messori – Diálogos sobre a Fé. Lisboa*: Verbo, 1985, p. 89–92. The Italian edition is: Joseph Ratzinger, Vittorio Messori – *Rapporto sulla fede* (Milão: Edizioni Paoline, 1985), p. 110–13.

third part of the secret, which he gives to Lucia for her to verify its authenticity.

- **5/13/2000** – Cardinal Sodano, Vatican Secretary of State at the end of the Eucharistic celebration presided by John Paul II, in which Francisco and Jacinta Marto were beatified, reveals, in Fatima, the content of the third part of the secret.
- **6/26/2000** – The Congregation for the Doctrine of the Faith publicly presents the third part of the secret of Fatima at a press conference headed by Cardinal Joseph Ratzinger, author of the theological commentary on the secret of Fatima.

The Contents of the Secret

With the timeline of the secret's revelation understood, we can rightfully ask, "Well, what was this secret?"

Remember the secret had three parts, so it was revealed to the children like a triptych piece of art (a piece of art depicted on three panels). This occurred during the July 13, 1917 apparition.

The first part was a dramatic vision of hell; the second part involved devotion to the Immaculate Heart of Mary in the context of an announcement of another war, famine, and persecution of the Church and the spread of communism; finally, the third part concerned the Church's pilgrimage towards Christ and the persecution she would face, as well as the suffering of the pope and that of the martyrs.

Here is how Lucia described each part.

Vision of Hell

As Our Lady spoke these last words, she opened her hands once more, as she had done during the two previous months. The rays of light seemed to penetrate the earth, and we saw as it were a sea of fire. Plunged in this fire were demons and souls in human form, like transparent burning embers, all blackened or burnished bronze, floating about in the conflagration, now raised into the air by the flames that issued from within themselves together with great clouds of smoke now falling back on every side like sparks in huge fires, without weight or equilibrium, amid shrieks and groans of pain and despair, which horrified us and made us tremble with fear. (It must have been this sight which caused me to cry out, as people say they heard me). The demons could be distinguished by their terrifying and repellent likeness to frightful and unknown animals, black and transparent like burning coals.[80]

Immaculate Heart of Mary in the Context of World Events

Terrified and as if to plead for succor, we looked up at Our Lady, who said to us, so kindly and so sadly: "You have seen hell where the souls of poor sinners go. To save them, God wishes to establish in the world

---

[80] Lucia de Jesus, *Fatima in Lucia's own words*, vol. 1. 22nd ed. (Fátima: Fundação Francisco e Jacinta Marto, 2018), p. 178.

devotion to my Immaculate Heart. If what I say to you is done, many souls will be saved and there will be peace. The war is going to end; but if people do not cease offending God, a worse one will break out during the pontificate of Pius XI. When you see a night illumined by an unknown light, know that this is the great sign given you by God that he is about to punish the world for its crimes, by means of war, famine, and persecutions of the Church and of the Holy Father. To prevent this, I shall come to ask for the consecration of Russia to my Immaculate Heart, and the Communion of Reparation on the First Saturdays. If my requests are heeded, Russia will be converted, and there will be peace; if not, she will spread her errors throughout the world, causing wars and persecutions of the Church. The good will be martyred, the Holy Father will have much to suffer, various nations will be annihilated. In the end, my Immaculate Heart will triumph. The Holy Father will consecrate Russia to me, and she will be converted, and a period of peace will be granted to the world. In Portugal, the dogma of the Faith will always be preserved."[81]

Persecution of the Church and the Holy Father

After the two parts which I have already explained, at the left of Our Lady and a little above, we saw an Angel with a flaming sword in his left hand; flashing, it gave out flames that looked as though they would set

---

[81]   Ibid., p. 178–79.

the world on fire; but they died out in contact with the splendor that Our Lady radiated towards him from her right hand: pointing to the earth with his right hand, the Angel cried out in a loud voice: "Penance, Penance, Penance!" And we saw in an immense light that is God—something similar to how people appear in a mirror when they pass in front of it—a Bishop dressed in White; we had the impression that it was the Holy Father. Other Bishops, Priests, men and women Religious were going up a steep mountain, at the top of which there was a big Cross of rough-hewn trunks as of a cork-tree with the bark; before reaching there the Holy Father passed through a big city half in ruins and half trembling with a halting step, afflicted with pain and sorrow, he prayed for the souls of the corpses he met on his way; having reached the top of the mountain, on his knees at the foot of the big Cross he was killed by a group of soldiers who fired bullets and arrows at him, and in the same way there died one after another the other Bishops, Priests, men and women Religious, and various lay people of different ranks and positions. Beneath the two arms of the Cross there were two Angels each with a crystal aspersorium in his hand, in which they gathered up the blood of the Martyrs and with it sprinkled the souls that were making their way to God.[82]

---

[82]   Ibid., p. 215.

The Theological Significance of the Secret

Now that we know the contents of the secret, it is important to discuss its theological implications. These visions were so sensational that they can be misconstrued if we are not careful.

Let us begin first with the vision of hell, which was revealed through an intense experience of God. Recall that Lucia said, "As Our Lady spoke these last words, she opened her hands once more, as she had done during the two previous months. The rays of light seemed to penetrate the earth." It is only through God's light that we understand all the depths of what was shown to the children in Fatima. Without the Holy Spirit, we will not understand anything that is presented to us through them.

Even knowing this, it is not easy to understand hell because it is a reality which is not within a temporal dimension but in a transcendental and eternal dimension. This forces us to rely on symbolic language, just as Jesus did when he wanted to explain the loss of or the moving away from God. He used words and human expressions like "fiery furnace," "eternal fire," "darkness," and "wailing and grinding of teeth" (Mt 13:42; 10:28).

The *Catechism of the Catholic Church* states that "the chief punishment of hell is eternal separation from God" and that the teaching about hell is "a call to the responsibility incumbent upon man to make use of his freedom in view of his eternal destiny" (CCC 1035–36).

For its part, theology teaches us that everything Sacred Scripture says about hell "is to be read according to the eschatological nature of the discourse, and not to be seen as a foretelling commentary . . . but as revealing the situation in which man actually finds himself."[83] In other words, hell is a pressing invitation for human beings to order their lives and take the choices they make seriously, because they face "the real possibility of eternal ruin," as Pope Benedict once put it.

Theology, though, cannot comment on the number of condemned souls, the type of punishment they receive, or the "geography" of hell, because the Gospels do not answer these questions. Revelation does not stipulate this, and *neither does Our Lady of Fatima.*

With that horrifying vision, Our Lady did not try to provide new information about hell, as if it were a color film about the world beyond, and even less did she want to frighten the children. What was shown was meant to provoke their consciences, calling them to a message of salvation. "You have seen hell where the souls of poor sinners go. To save them, God wishes to establish in the world devotion to my Immaculate Heart. If what I say to you is done, many souls will be saved and there will be peace."[84]

Here we have that dual denouncing and annunciation element of this prophetic message, a warning of judgement and the possibility of radical destruction, but also the promise of salvation through a given means: in this case, devotion to the Immaculate Heart of Mary.

In the vision and through her words, Our Lady highlights the reality of our free will and the importance of the choices

---

[83]   Karl Rahner, Hell, in Sacramnetum Mundi, 553–54.

[84]   Cf. Stefano de Fiores, O segredo de Fatima. In COUTINHO, Vítor (coord.). *Mensagem de Esperança para o mundo: Acontecimento e significado de Fatima* (Fatima: Santuário de Fatima, 2012), p. 121–23.

we make. Above all, she helps us recognize that we can be personally responsible for helping souls avoid the horrors of hell.

Lucia describes her understanding on this matter, saying, "Whatever the true state of affairs, what is certain is that hell exists, and it is something about which Our Lady is greatly concerned. This is clear from her Message, in which She asks several times for prayers and sacrifices for the conversion of sinners: 'You have seen hell where the souls of poor sinners go. To save them, God wishes to establish in the world devotion to my Immaculate Heart.'"[85]

The vision of hell awoke in particular the charism of Francisco and Jacinta to become aware of what they could do to save souls. Jacinta felt a deep sorrow for sinners from this day forward. It's amazing how she adopted the poor sinners as her own. She saw it as her mission to save sinners by means of prayer and sacrifice.

In one moment, Lucia tells us:

> At other times, after thinking for a while, she said: "So many people falling into hell! So many people in hell!"
>
> To quieten her, I said: "Don't be afraid! You're going to Heaven."
>
> "Yes, I am," she said serenely, "but I want all those people to go there too!"[86]

---

[85]   Lucia de Jesus, *The message of Fatima: How I see the Message in the Course of time and in the Light of Events* (Fatima: Carmelo de Coimbra; Secretariado dos Pastorinhos, 2006), p. 50.
Lucia de Jesus, *Fatima in Lucia's own words*, p. 126.

Francisco, for his part, was attentive to the sorrow of God over losing his children like this. He and Jacinta and Lucia did not become traumatized children after the vision of hell. They were unusually realistic and motivated children, free from selfishness, uncommon at their age. With a keen awareness of the meaning of their existence, they became more responsible, more generous, more willing to do everything they could to save souls.

The second part of the secret leaves the eternal realm behind to dive into a more historical and political appeal. It refers to wars and famine, and to persecution of the Church and the pope. Our Lady attributes a harmful effect of Russia that will spread its errors throughout the world and destroy several nations.

On the one hand, Russia is a people, a historical power unknown to the children. But on the other hand, it symbolically represents the explicit refusal of God on a political and social level. These two aspects cannot be confused or thought of as the same. In a prudent and balanced way, we can interpret the second part of the secret with this distinction in mind.

In Russia, Communism resulted in the death of millions, many of which were Catholic, and destroyed the independence of many nations. As John Paul II said, we can verify in this dynamic "the willingness and the systematic program of the destruction of all that entails religion!" [87]

---

[87]   Quoted by Luciano Guerra, in "*Fatima e o século breve*", in CON-GRESSO INTERNACIONAL, Fátima para o século XXI (Fáti-ma: Santuário de Fátima, 2008), 457–84, 468. The author registers these words said by the pope during an audience with the bishop of Leiria-Fatima, when he hands him the bullet of the attack.

This cannot, however, be used to demonize a whole country and its people. There are authors, like Stefano De Fiores, who defend Russia as a more historical reference with its role in worldwide geopolitics. For J. M. Alonso, Russia did not have a geographical connotation but rather a moral and religious one, being merely a symbolic name for the evil opposition to God and the Church. We must find a balance when trying to understand these two dimensions, historical and symbolic, without absolutizing either one.

Lucia would later see Russia as a symbol for all those who try to eradicate God. What worried Our Lady was its atheistic philosophy. She was denouncing all the totalitarian systems that, in any way, are an obstacle to people living their faith. This goes for communism, but also materialism, secularism, hedonism, and any other form of totalitarian government or philosophy that seeks to lessen or destroy the values of faith.

To avoid all of this, Our Lord wishes to establish in the world devotion to the Immaculate Heart of Mary. Our Lady said, "I shall come to ask for the consecration of Russia to my Immaculate Heart, and the Communion of Reparation on the First Saturdays."

The specifics of this devotion will be chronicled in the next chapter, but we underline here the solution God offered to prevent wars, famine, persecution of the Church, and the atheistic philosophy at the foundation of communism. This solution is found not only in keeping the commandments but also in a spirituality that harmonizes with the Immaculate Heart of Mary.

And now we move to the theological significance of the third part of the secret. Here, we have to recall that, like the other two parts, the language Our Lady uses is symbolic and prophetic.

Let's review what the children saw. First, in the beginning, they saw an angel with a flaming sword trying to touch the Earth. But the angel could do no harm to the world because the Blessed Mother was there. With her right hand, she was preventing the flames from touching the Earth.

In the theological commentary of the third part of the secret, Cardinal Ratzinger presented the Church's interpretation of this. (Lucia did not presume to give her own interpretation, feeling as though she was merely the one given the vision but it was up to the Church to interpret it.)

Cardinal Ratzinger explains, "This represents the threat of judgement which looms over the world. Today the prospect that the world might be reduced to ashes by a sea of fire no longer seems pure fantasy: man himself, with his inventions, has forged the flaming sword. The vision then shows the power which stands opposed to the force of destruction— the splendor of the Mother of God and, stemming from this in a certain way, the summons to penance."[88]

Ratzinger saw the flaming sword not as a metaphor for God punishing us but as a metaphor of what man himself had invented—namely, the atomic bomb. Who created this? Not God but humanity.

The angel's utterance of, "Penance, Penance, Penance!" is also significant. This is the first time this word is mentioned

---

[88]   Joseph Ratzinger, *The Message of Fatima*, Congregation for the Doctrine of Faith, June 2000.

in the narrative of Fatima. According to the official explanation of the Church: "The key word of this third part is the threefold cry: 'Penance, Penance, Penance!' The beginning of the Gospel comes to mind: 'Repent and believe the Good News' (Mk 1:15). To understand the signs of the times means to accept the urgency of penance—of conversion—of faith."[89]

Lucia, later in her life, said, "But what penance is it that God asks of us? To begin with, the sacrifice that each one has to impose on him or herself in order to leave the way of sin and embark on a path of honesty, purity, justice, truth and love."[90]

After the angel, the children saw many other things: a cross on top of a mountain, a city half in ruins, a pilgrimage of people, the pope, the martyrs, angels collecting the blood of the martyr, and the presence of the woman more shining than the sun.

Let us consider each of these aspects individually.

A Cross on Top of a Mountain

They saw a group of people of all kinds walking and climbing a steep mountain with a cross at the top. These people were led by the pope, so this can be seen as the pilgrimage of the Church going to the cross, towards Christ, the end of history. Christ is the goal of our journey and our strength to get there. Ratzinger wrote, "On the mountain stands the cross — the goal and guide of history. The cross transforms

---

[89]   Ibid.

[90]   Lucia de Jesus, *The message of Fatima*, p. 29.

destruction into salvation; it stands as a sign of history's misery but also as a promise for history."[91]

Jesus is there, in the center of the third part of the secret, as the end of our pilgrimage. The big question that arises from this is: What am I doing with my life? Am I walking to the cross? Or am I running away from it?

A City Half in Ruins

But before climbing the steep mountain and going to the cross, they have to pass through a city half in ruins. The prefect of the Congregation for the Doctrine of Faith explains, "The mountain and city symbolize the arena of human history: history as an arduous ascent to the summit, history as the arena of human creativity and social harmony, but at the same time a place of destruction, where man actually destroys the fruits of his own work. The city can be the place of communion and progress, but also of danger and the most extreme menace."[92]

Our current pontiff, Francis, describes the Church as a field hospital after battle. He says we must go out and look for the wounded. This message helped my own personal understanding of the third part of the secret. The Church, before getting to Christ, has to assume the wounds of our civilization as we pass through the city in ruins. If we do not touch the wounds of our brothers and sisters—not only the physical wounds but also the wounds of the soul—we do

---

[91]   Joseph Ratzinger, *The Message of Fatima*, Congregation for the Doctrine of Faith, June 2000.

[92]   Ibid.

not understand anything about the One who hangs on that cross!

We are called to touch these wounds as Jesus did, with mercy and kindness. Fatima challenges us to take on the ruins of our time with courage, with hope, and with tremendous love for Jesus and for the wounded ones. We are called to be there.

When Pope Francis went to Fatima on May 13, 2017 for the celebration of the centennial of the apparitions and the canonization of Francisco and Jacinta, he did something that people couldn't help notice. Usually, when the pope enters the Shrine of Fatima, he goes towards the Little Chapel by car. But when Pope Francis entered for the candle procession, he came on foot. I immediately thought of the "bishop dressed in white" who walks with the church described in the secret. The pope walks with his people. It was an amazing moment, an amazing gesture, walking in the middle of the crowd holding all those candles.

A Pilgrimage of People

When we speak of the "pilgrimage of the Church," how do we know that this is the Catholic Church? One indication is that the pilgrimage is being led by the pope. If you take him away, the procession could be any group of Christians. The presence of "the bishop dressed in white" clearly shows the scene is meant to refer to the Catholic Church. Cardinal Ratzinger interprets the presence of "the bishop dressed in white," saying:

The Pope seems to precede the others, trembling and suffering because of all the horrors around him. Not only do the houses of the city lie half in ruins, but he makes his way among the corpses of the dead. The Church's path is thus described as a *Via Crucis*, as a journey through a time of violence, destruction and persecution. The history of an entire century can be seen represented in this image. Just as the places of the earth are synthetically described in the two images of the mountain and the city, and are directed towards the cross, so too time is presented in a compressed way.[93]

To understand the objective of the journey—this pilgrimage—is to understand the identity of the Church. The pilgrims' gaze is upon the cross as they go through a city in ruins. The cross gives hope and keeps them marching through the ruins without weakening. To the extent that the Church identifies itself with the cross and with the Crucified Jesus, she can inspire hope in the ruins of the civilization she inhabits.

The Pope

The figure of the pope appears frequently in the matters concerning Fatima, especially in the third part of the secret and in two of Jacinta's visions. In hindsight, the identity of the "bishop dressed in white" is clear, but when he was mentioned to the children more than one hundred years ago, they would not have understood who this figure was. Only

---

[93]   Ibid.

once it was explained to them did they begin to have a great love for the Holy Father, offering their sacrifices and prayers for him and for his intentions.

Little Jacinta was especially ardent in this respect. Lucia tells us of her cousin's "meetings" with the pope:

> One day we spent our siesta down by my parents' well. Jacinta sat on the stone slabs on top of the well. Francisco and I climbed up a steep bank in search of wild honey among the brambles in a nearby thicket. After a little while, Jacinta called out to me: "Didn't you see the Holy Father?"
>
> "No."
>
> "I don't know how it was, but I saw the Holy Father in a very big house, kneeling by a table, with his head buried in his hands, and he was weeping. Outside the house, there were many people. Some of them were throwing stones, others were cursing him and using bad language. Poor Holy Father, we must pray very much for him."

On another occasion, Lucia recalls, "We went to the cave called Loca do Cabeço. As soon as we got there, we prostrated on the ground, saying the prayers the Angel had taught us. After some time, Jacinta stood up and called to me: 'Can't you see all those highways and roads and fields full of people, who are crying with hunger and have nothing to eat? And the Holy Father in a church praying before the

Immaculate Heart of Mary? And so many people praying with him?'" [94]

In these visions, the pope was not named and the focus was on his role as pontiff, as intercessor for the faithful. Thus, it appears the pope in the scenes that Jacinta saw was not so much one individual but the person who serves as *the* pope, the successor of St. Peter, no matter who he is. Given the nature of the times in which we live, a time of great confusion and relativism about this matter, it seems providential that the Fatima message emphasizes the importance of love for the Holy Father and the duty we have to pray for him.

Jacinta prayed so much for the pope and made so many sacrifices that when John Paul II beatified her, he said in his homily, "I also express my gratitude to Blessed Jacinta for the sacrifices and prayers offered for the Holy Father, whom she saw suffering greatly."[95] Pope Benedict XVI, during his visit to Fatima on May 13, 2010, also thanked the shepherd children for all the love they showed the Holy Father.

The Angels Collecting the Blood of the Martyrs

Significantly, the Fatima vision in which the pope appears also depicts the martyrs of the Church, of which there have been more in the twentieth and twenty-first centuries than in any others.

As then Cardinal Ratzinger put it, "In the vision we . . . recognize the last century as a century of martyrs, a century of suffering and persecution for the Church, a century of

---

94   Lucia de Jesus, *Fatima in Lucia's own words*, p. 128–29.

95   John Paulo II, Homily, Shrine of Fatima, May 13, 2000, Beatification of Francisco and Jacinta.

World Wars and the many local wars which filled the last fifty years and have inflicted unprecedented forms of cruelty."[96]

Nonetheless, the cardinal insists that this *Via Crucis* (Way of the Cross) is a way of hope, consolation, and life:

> It is a consoling vision, which seeks to open a history of blood and tears to the healing power of God. Beneath the arms of the cross angels gather up the blood of the martyrs, and with it they give life to the souls making their way to God. Here, the blood of Christ and the blood of the martyrs are considered as one: the blood of the martyrs runs down from the arms of the cross. The martyrs die in communion with the Passion of Christ, and their death becomes one with his. For the sake of the body of Christ, they complete what is still lacking in his afflictions (cf. Col 1:24). Their life has itself become a Eucharist, part of the mystery of the grain of wheat which in dying yields abundant fruit. The blood of the martyrs is the seed of Christians, said Tertullian. As from Christ's death, from his wounded side, the Church was born, so the death of the witnesses is fruitful for the future life.[97]

As Cardinal Ratzinger's words make clear, the message of Fatima states that if we are willing to imitate Christ and make our lives a gift to others so that they may have life, each of our crosses will bear abundant fruit.

---

[96]   Joseph Ratzinger, *The Message of Fatima*, Congregation for the Doctrine of Faith, June 2000.

[97]   Ibid.

The Presence of the Woman More Shining Than the Sun

One of the most visually beautiful and spiritually meaningful parts of the vision is "the presence of the woman more shining than the sun." Lucia movingly describes that everything in the vision took place in the presence and under the maternal care of the Mother of God, "with the splendor that Our Lady radiated towards him [the angel with the flaming sword] from her right hand."

Once again, Our Lady is described as full of light and splendor. Her presence offers us not only the reassuring certainty of her care throughout our earthly journey (cf. LG 62) but most importantly offers us the key to understanding the history of the Church, which is, from her very beginnings, to follow Christ crucified. This implies necessarily to face atheist and repressive systems. As Benedict says, "In the *via crucis* of the Church's history, Christians who travel the steep road towards the heavenly Jerusalem for full communion with the living God must go through 'the city in ruins' where they will often be persecuted and martyred. The sacrificial dimension filled with a love for Jesus and on behalf of sinners as well as for the pope marked so many of the actions and prayers of the three seers of Fatima, who joyfully completed in their flesh what is lacking in the afflictions of Christ on behalf of his body, which is the Church (cf. Col. 1:24)."[98]

---

[98]   Franco Manzi, O inferno, Nossa Senhora e o papa na visão de 13 de julho de 1917. Tentativa de discernimento eclesial. In GOMES Pedro Valinho (coord.). *Segredo: liturgia de Palavra, silêncio e testemunho. Aproximações polissémicas ao segredo de Fátima* (Fátima: Santuário de Fátima, 2018), p. 188–89.

The Secret's Relevance for Today

The Fatima story, the apparitions, and the secret give rise to at least two questions. First: Have these prophecies been fulfilled? Second: What do they have to do with my own life today?

In the following passage, Cardinal Ratzinger helps us understand the lasting effect of the secret and how we must view it today. He speaks of the primacy of our freedom and of our ability to change the future through our actions. He invites us not to view these visions as a prophecy of a predetermined and definitive future but as events and circumstances we can keep from happening. In this way, he emphasizes that the grim visions of what could come to pass should be seen more as a warning than as a prediction:

> The vision then shows the power which stands opposed to the force of destruction—the splendor of the Mother of God and, stemming from this in a certain way, the summons to penance. In this way, the importance of human freedom is underlined: the future is not in fact unchangeably set, and the image which the children saw is in no way a film preview of a future in which nothing can be changed. Indeed, the whole point of the vision is to bring freedom onto the scene and to steer freedom in a positive direction. The purpose of the vision is not to show a film of an irrevocably fixed future. Its meaning is exactly the opposite: it is meant to mobilize the forces of change in the right

direction. Therefore we must totally discount fatalistic
explanations of the "secret."[99]

Like so many writers who have tackled this subject, I believe
that the "most prophetic of the modern apparitions" is
related to not only the Church's past but also to its present
and future. We have been given an exhortation, just as the
people of the Old Testament had on so many occasions, of
what a life without God will look like. It is our call to ensure
this doesn't come to pass.

As Our Lady makes clear, our faith, our prayers, and our
sacrifices can help to avoid disatrous situations and to save
souls that otherwise would be lost: "If what I say to you is
done, there will be peace, many souls will be saved, if not
then . . ."

The presence of the words *if* and *then* calls us to the
responsible use of our freedom. By saying "if," she implies
that we can significantly influence what happens. Our Lady
assures us that our individual lives matter and that our personal holiness is decisive not only for our own lives but for
that of others, for our country, for our world, and for our
Church.

Some have speculated that the attack on John Paul II
on May 13, 1981—the assassination attempt on "a bishop
dressed in white"—brought a close to the vision's purpose.
After all, this event seemed to be an explicit manifestation of
what the children had seen in the vision. Pope John Paul II
himself also understood the clear connection, claiming that

---

[99]   Joseph Ratzinger, *The Message of Fatima*, Congregation for the
Doctrine of Faith, June 2000.

during the attack there was a special and miraculous intervention by Our Lady. With her "maternal hand," she lead the "trajectory of the bullet," not allowing it to go beyond the "threshold of death."[100]

However, most Fatima theologians write that all of the popes of the twentieth and twenty-first centuries are archetypically represented by the "bishop dressed in white," and that all of them need the intercessory prayer of the faithful. Pope Benedict XVI suggested this ongoing character of the secret when, at Fatima, he said, "We would be mistaken to think that Fatima's prophetic mission is complete."[101]

The Core of the Secret

We have dissected much pertaining to this secret. If we are not careful, we can get lost in the conversation and, in frustration, write the whole thing off as a dramatic and confusing event that flies above our own ordinary lives and capacities.

To avoid this temptation, let us boil down the core of the secret and what it means for the Church in the twenty-first century into three points:

---

[100]   John Paul II, "La meditazione com l'episcopato italiano raccolto nella Basilica di Santa Maria Maggiore per la recita del rosário [Venerdì, 13 maggio 1994]", em Id., *Insegnamenti di Giovanni Paolo II*, XVII-1, 1994 (gennaio-giugno), Libreria Editrice Vaticana, Città del Vaticano 1994, 1058-1064: 1061". Quoted by Franco Manzi, O inferno, Nossa Senhora e o papa na visão de 13 de julho de 1917. Tentativa de discernimento eclesial. In GOMES Pedro Valinho (coord.). *Segredo: liturgia de Palavra, silêncio e testemunho. Aproximações polissémicas ao segredo de Fátima* (Fátima: Santuário de Fátima, 2018), p. 189.

[101]   Benedict XVI, *Homily*, Fatima, May 13, 2010.

1. Fatima urges us to accept our responsibility, which derives from our freedom, recognizing that each of us plays an essential role in what happens in the world and in history.

2. Fatima calls us, through our prayers and sacrifices, to do all we can to heal the wounds of those living amidst the ruins of a civilization enclosed in its multiple forms of selfishness.

3. Fatima assures us that God continues to take care of our journey and invites us to hope and trust.

The Secret's Conclusion

Much has been said and debated about whether the secret has been fully revealed, and if more events will come to pass concerning it. Others have said that the consecration of the world to the Immaculate Heart of Mary has yet to be done successfully. Lucia disagrees.

On November 17, 2001, Cardinal Bertone, secretary for the Congregation of the Doctrine of Faith, met with her in the Carmel of Coimbra. In the course of the conversation, she confirmed that the third part of the secret had already been revealed and that the consecration to the Immaculate Heart of Mary, done on March 25, 1984 by John Paul II "had been accepted in heaven." As a follow-up to this conversation, a document was drawn up to establish the content of the conversation. This was signed by the two parties before being published in the weekly Portuguese edition of the *L'Osservatore Romano* newspaper.

On May 21, 2016, Pope Emeritus Benedict XVI reinforced Lucia's belief, publicly stating that the secret of Fatima had been completely revealed.[102]

The Power of Prayer and Trust

When Cardinal Ratzinger came to Fatima in 1996, he spoke movingly of the importance of prayer and on the power of simple and "hidden" things being able to change the world: "It seems to me that our biggest mistake is to think that only great economic and political actions can transform the world. It is a strong temptation even among Christians, to think that prayer lacks value, and therefore interiority is lost. Now here in Fatima we hear about hidden things, such as conversions, prayer, penance, that seem to have no political significance, but they are the crucial things. They are the renewing power of the world."[103]

We often feel powerless to combat the evil in our world, but Ratzinger's words serve as a reminder that there is great power in prayer. The message of Fatima urges us never to lose hope in our ability to take an active role in the salvation of the world, even when we kneel at our bedside in the quiet darkness of our rooms.

And finally, there is a curious aspect to the secret we have not yet touched upon: that of trust. This has to do not so much with the content or theological meaning of the secret

---

[102]   See the link: https:// press.vatican.va/content/salastampa/it/bollettino/pubblico/2016/05/21/0366/00855.html (12/29/2019).

[103]   Aura Miguel, *O segredo que conduz o Papa. A experiência de Fátima no Pontificado de João Paulo II* (2.a ed.), (São João do Estoril: Principia, 2000), 143–44.

but how it affected the lives of the seers. It was this secret that made them suffer the most, what gave them so many trials and grievances. It led to their imprisonment and to violent threats of torture.

Yet through their faith in Our Lady, who had asked them to say nothing to anyone, they accepted even the possibility of their own death. They would rather have died than betray the trust of the Lady brighter than the sun.

We may not have our lives put on the line, but we should live with this same level of devotion to God and his mother. We must know that despite the chaos and pain, they are still with us, and if we remain faithful to what they ask of us, rest assured that the miraculous is possible.

CHAPTER 7

The Immaculate Heart of Mary

How Do We View Our Lady?

In one of her books, Sister Lucia describes her first encounter with Our Lady: "It was on May 13th, 1917, just after midday, when the Heavenly Messenger, wrapped in the light of God which transforms her, as if she was a new creature, came down from heaven to earth, in order to bring us the message which God had entrusted to her, to come down to his own children to whom Jesus had entrusted to her care when in agony on the Cross."[104]

Who is this woman dressed "in the light of God which transforms her"? What can she teach us about the God who sent her, and about ourselves, about our dignity and our mission?

A wide range of literature has been devoted to this woman in the last two millennia. Some surprising articles have appeared even in the secular sphere, including a *National*

---

[104] Lucia de Jesus, *The message of Fatima: how I see the Message in the course of time and in the light of events* (Fátima: Carmelo de Coimbra; Secretariado dos Pastorinhos, 2006), p. 27.

Geographic from December of 2015 with the cover story "Mary: The Most Powerful Woman in the World."

When Pope Francis visited Fatima for the canonization of Francisco and Jacinta, he spoke about how we view Mary, asking if she is "a teacher of the spiritual life, the first to follow Jesus on the 'narrow way' of the cross by giving us an example, or a Lady 'unapproachable' and impossible to imitate? A woman 'blessed because she believed' always and everywhere in God's words (cf. Lk 1:42.45), or a 'plaster statue' from whom we beg favors at little cost?"[105]

In other words, how do we see her?

On the one hand, we may forget that, above all, she is a woman, a human being like us. We place her on a pedestal, and rightfully so, but in doing so, we sometimes make her a distant figure. We forget that she is "one of us" and someone we can imitate as a disciple of Christ. If we only focus on her privileges (her immaculate conception, her assumption into heaven, her status as the Mother of God), she can certainly seem unapproachable, even intimidating.

Another danger is to approach her, as the pope said, merely to "beg favors at little cost." She is our intercessor with her Son, but she is no wish-granter.

So where do we stand? How are we to view her? The role of the Immaculate Heart of Mary in the Fatima apparitions helps give us our answer.

---

[105]   Francis, *Blessing of the Candles*, Shrine of Fatima, May 12, 2017, Canonization of Francisco and Jacinta.

Cova da Iria on the day of the miracle of the sun.

Cova da Iria, October 13, 1917.

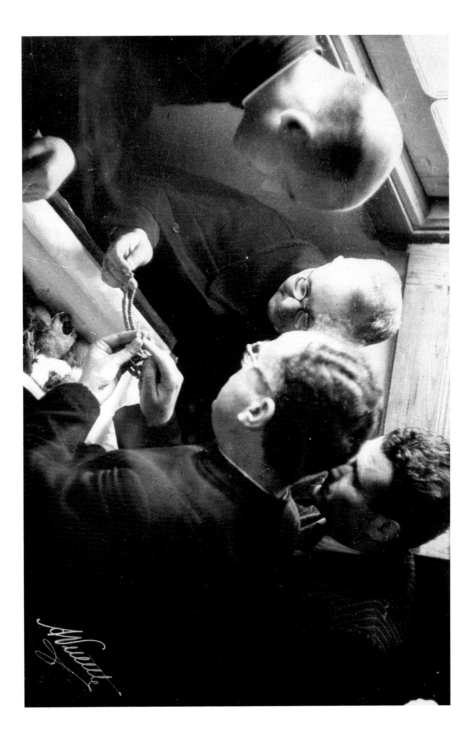

Above: Jacinta's incorrupt body after the opening of her coffin on
September 12, 1935.
Left: The recognition of Francisco's mortal remains and the rosary
which was buried with him.

The house where Francisco and Jacinta were born and where Francisco died in Aljustrel.

The house of Lucia's parents in Aljustrel.

The little shepherds at the site of the apparitions.

The three little shepherds. Photograph taken by Fr. Joel in the garden of Francisco and Jacinta's home.

The little shepherds at the site of the apparitions, taken after the miracle of the sun.

Lucia and Jacinta – September 1917.

Photograph of the little shepherds taken in Francisco and Jacinta's orchard and published in the paper *O Seculo*.

The little shepherds at the site of the apparitions on
October 13, 1917.

Loca do Cabeço where Lucia, Francisco, and Jacinta had the first and third apparitions of the angel in 1916.

Monument commemorating the second apparition of the angel at the well of Lucia's garden.

Monument commemorating the third apparition
of the angel at Loca do Cabeço.

The well belonging to Lucia's parents, meeting-place of the
little shepherds and where the second apparition of the angel
took place. Here Jacinta also had another vision of the pope.

Above: Valinhos, the site of the fourth apparition of Our Lady, on August 19, 1917.
Below: The parish church of Fatima at the time of the apparitions. Here the little shepherds were baptized.

Maria Aurea and Maria Clara, founders of Aliança de Santa Maria.

Sisters of Aliança de Santa Maria.

Sr. Angela meeting with Pope Benedict XVI on May 13, 2010 at the
Shrine of Fatima.

Sr. Angela meeting with Pope Francis on May 13, 2017 at the Shrine of Fatima for the canonization of Francisco and Jacinta.

The canonizations of Saints Francisco and Jacinta on May 13, 1917. Sr. Angela and Dr. Pedro Valinho holding the relics of Francisco and Jacinta.

The Logic of God and Our Lady

At the beginning of the apparitions, Lucia asked Our Lady where she was from, which is another way of asking *who* she is. Our Lady did not answer but rather made a request: "I have come to ask you to come here six months in succession on the thirteenth day, at this same hour. Later on, I will tell you who I am and what I want."[106]

What a strange way to start a meeting! When we are introduced to other people, the first thing we usually say is our name. Not Our Lady. She first asks for six encounters. Mary seems to be implying that Lucia can know the Blessed Mother's identity best by developing a relationship with her.

This manner of proceeding inverts the usual "logic" of our lives. Usually, we want to know and understand everything before we decide to accept it or not. We use this logic in our earthly lives and often apply the same reasoning to the things of God. But the things of God don't always work according to our rules and regulations. Often, he asks for faith *first*, and only then does he offer us the understanding we seek.

The founder of my order, who later became my superior, explained this reversal of human logic very well when I wanted to understand everything about God, about the vocational process, and about faith. She used to say, "Angela, this is not mathematics. In math, we know A+B=C. If I know A and B and the relation between them, then I can conclude C. With God, sometimes the process operates the

---

[106]   Lucia de Jesus, *Fatima in Lucia's own words*, vol. 1, 22nd ed. (Fátima: Fundação Francisco e Jacinta Marto, 2018), p. 175.

other way around. We accept C, and with time, he explains A and B."

Our Lady uses the same procedure: "I want you to come here. *Then* I will explain who I am." As a prelude to their meetings and their relationship, she asks the children to have faith. By extension, Mary asks the same of all her children. Through such faith, we can come to know her better and understand what she asks of us.

For example, Mary asks us to pray the Rosary. Whoever wants to understand the importance of the Rosary before starting to pray it will never even begin. Once we start praying it, we discover its beauty and efficacy. Likewise, those who need to understand all the particulars of the First Saturday Devotion beforehand will never start. Yet when we start doing it, *then* we understand this devotion and develop a love for it (and then we don't want to stop!).

You might say Our Lady appeals to the "intelligence of the heart." With some things, the heart must understand before the mind does. So to understand the Immaculate Heart of Mary, I ask you to open up your own heart and trust in its power.

The Immaculate Heart of Mary in the Apparitions

Devotion to the Immaculate Heart of Mary goes back to ancient times in the Church. The first scriptural reference to the heart of Mary comes from the Gospel of Luke when he tells us that she "kept all these things, pondering them in her heart" (Lk 2:19, 51), these things concerning the mysteries of Christ's birth in Bethlehem and the story of his being lost for three days before being found in the Temple in Jerusalem.

From the early Church Fathers through the Middle Ages, devotion to the Heart of Mary underwent a profound development, especially with St. John Eudes in the seventeenth century, but also with others.

What we see in Fatima builds off this foundation but offers a new perspective at the same time. There is a specific and strong emphasis on the *Immaculate Heart of Mary* in Fatima, but the iconography differs from previous styles. Before Fatima, the iconography related to the Heart of Mary was centered around a depiction of the name of the Sacred Heart of Mary, and the elements that constituted this iconography were flowers, swords, or a flame. The Immaculate Heart of Mary, meanwhile, is shown only with thorns surrounding the heart.

A quick examination of the times when the Immaculate Heart of Mary is present in the message of Fatima shows how central a role Mary's heart plays in the apparitions. Her Immaculate Heart appears or is referred to on the following occasions:

1. The first apparition of the angel, spring of 1916
2. The second apparition of the angel, summer of 1916
3. The third apparition of the angel, autumn of 1916
4. Apparition of Our Lady, June 13, 1917
5. Apparition of Our Lady, July 13, 1917
6. Apparition of Our Lord and Our Lady at Pontevedra, December 10, 1925
7. Apparition at Tui, June 13, 1929

There is not enough time and space to adequately cover all these, but discussing the significance of a few of them will shed important light on the role of the Immaculate Heart of Mary in the Fatima message.

The Angel Speaks of the Heart of Mary

In the first apparition of the angel in the spring of 1916, he said, "Pray thus. The Hearts of Jesus and Mary are attentive to the voice of your supplications."[107]

From the beginning, we see here that the Heart of Mary is presented in union with the Heart of Jesus. This already says something theologically about what the Immaculate Heart of Mary is in Fatima. It is always united to the Heart of Jesus, always listening to our prayers along with him.

In times of trial, people often say, "Sister, it seems as if God is no longer listening to me." My friends, it isn't true! God always listens! He may sometimes not answer the way we would like, or when and how we want, but there is never a prayer rising from a broken or wounded heart that God does not hear. Grace always comes to a heart that prays, even if we do not understand the grace we receive. The Sacred Scriptures assure us of this, and the angel repeats it in Fatima, telling us that God is "attentive to the voice of your supplications."

During the second apparition of the angel in the summer of 1916, he again points to the union of the two hearts but adds a note about mercy. "The Hearts of Jesus and Mary have designs of mercy on you."[108]

Some say that God loves us as we are, which he does, but in fact he dreams bigger for us than we do for ourselves.

---

[107]   Lucia de Jesus, *Fatima in Lucia's own words*, p. 170.
[108]   Ibid., p. 171.

He has "designs of mercy" planned for us. Thus, we can ask God: How are you dreaming of me today?

The Hearts of Jesus and Mary have designs of mercy, an expectation, a vocation, a bigger project. Fatima speaks of the richness of our vocation, our "life project." We are so much more than what we sometimes want to make of our lives. We put limits on ourselves because we don't see ourselves with God's eyes.

Lucia underlines this: "God's designs of mercy are not restricted to the humble little shepherds. He has designs of mercy, grace, forgiveness and love for each one of us."[109]

In the third apparition of the angel in autumn of 1916, he says, "And, through the infinite merits of His most Sacred Heart, and the Immaculate Heart of Mary, I beg of you the conversion of poor sinners."[110]

These words in the last apparition of the angel serve as a prayer he taught the children. In it, the Blessed Mother is presented as the one who, with Jesus, intercedes for us, poor sinners, as she interceded in Cana.

With these three apparitions, the angel began the story of Fatima. And as we can see, in each, he stressed how important the Immaculate Heart of Mary is, chiefly because it is always in union with the Heart of Jesus.

Of the inseparability of these two hearts, Sister Lucia said, "Thus, in the closest union possible between two human beings, Christ began, with Mary, the work of our salvation.

---

[109]   Lucia de Jesus, *The message of Fatima: how I see the Message in the course of time and in the light of events* (Fátima: Carmelo de Coimbra; Secretariado dos Pastorinhos, 2006), p. 21.

[110]   Lucia de Jesus, *Fatima in Lucia's own words*, 2018, p. 173.

The Christ's heart-beats are those of the heart of Mary, the prayer of Christ is the prayer of Mary, the joys of Christ are the joys of Mary."[111]

The Immaculate Heart Is Our Refuge

Despite the importance of the angel's words, Our Lady's apparition in June of 1917 was the moment when the role and mission of the Immaculate Heart of Mary in the life of the shepherd children, especially Lucia, became more luminous and fundamental.

To understand what occurred then, we have to go back to the end of the previous apparition, following the children through the month of May and into June.

In the first apparition on May 13, Mary asked the children, "Are you willing to offer yourselves to God and bear all the sufferings He wills to send you, as an act of reparation for the sins by which He is offended, and of supplication for the conversion of sinners?"

They answered, "Yes, we are willing."

Then Our Lady replied, "Then you are going to have much to suffer, but the grace of God will be your comfort."[112]

Lucia was probably not expecting that the sufferings would start that very day!

After the May apparition, the children were full of joy. But Lucia asked her two cousins not to say anything about what they had seen and heard. Jacinta assured Lucia that she

---

would say nothing, but this promise evaporated as soon as she saw her mother.

Francisco and Jacinta's parents believed them, but Lucia's mother, Maria Rosa, a good woman in her own right, could not believe that such grace was granted to her child and to her family. Convinced it was all a lie, she grew fearful that her daughter was deceiving people. She was troubled still more when Lucia began to pray in front of the tree. And finally, she was grieved by the economic loss for the family, since the best farming grounds were precisely those in the Cova da Iria, the ones the pilgrims would totally destroy in the months to come. The family was already poor, but now they would be even more poverty-stricken.

Her mother tried everything to get Lucia to change her story and admit the apparitions didn't happen, including smacking her. This was an incredible suffering for a ten-year-old. We can imagine she was also confused. Her life had seemed more or less ideal until the apparitions, yet after them, confusion, suffering, and eventually persecution plagued her. Who would have thought that seeing the Blessed Mother would make one's life "worse"?

This led to a request from Lucia the very next month: "I would like to ask you to take us to Heaven."[113] It wasn't a longing for heaven that prompted this plea but a desire to make all the controversy go away. Before, she had been loved. Now, she was scolded, mocked, accused, misunderstood.

We are so used to thinking of God as a God of peace that it scandalizes us when the opposite happens. But God's ways are not our ways. As the prophet Isaiah said, "For my

---

[113]   Ibid., p. 177.

thoughts are not your thoughts, neither are your ways my ways, says the LORD" (Is 55:8–9).

Our Lady answered Lucia's request, though not in the way she had hoped: "Yes. I will take Jacinta and Francisco soon. But you are to stay here some time longer. Jesus wishes to make use of you to make me known and loved. He wants to establish in the world devotion to my Immaculate Heart. I promise salvation to those who embrace it, and those souls will be loved by God like flowers placed by me to adorn His throne."[114]

"Some time longer" turned out to be eighty-seven years! But what a mission Lucia would fulfill over those almost nine decades: to follow the will of God by spreading devotion to the Immaculate Heart of Mary.

But in that moment, as a little girl, all she heard was that her little cousins would soon die. These were not just members of her family but the only people who were experiencing this phenomenon with her, the only ones who truly understood. Such suffering she had to endure!

Here is how Lucia recalled this moment many years later: "This was the Mission which God had destined for me. But to remain on earth without the companionship of Jacinta and Francisco made it seem that I would be alone in this deserted and uncertain world, with no-one who could follow me, understand me, help and share things with me, treading with me the paths along which God wished to lead me."[115]

So, she replied, full of sadness, "Am I to stay here alone?"[116]

---

[114]   Ibid., p. 177.
[115]   Lucia de Jesus, *The message of Fatima*, p. 43.
[116]   Lucia de Jesus, *Fatima in Lucia's own words*, p. 177.

Here, Lucia asks Our Lady about the great suffering of our time: *loneliness.* This is a feeling that we all have at some point in our lives. Loneliness is not just about physical companionship; in fact, that is only a small part of it. People can feel lonely with many around them. The loneliness that tortures us is the interior loneliness when we feel that no one understands us and no one loves us. Sometimes we might even think God has abandoned us.

Loneliness is a common human experience. That is why Jesus assumed it in his own life. His disciples didn't understand him and his mission. They abandoned him in so many different ways. Even on the cross, Jesus cries out, "My God my God, why have you forsaken me?" (Mt 27:46)

I do not know your name, dear reader. I do not know what dwells in you. Your pains, your joys, your expectations, your suffering, your passions, your failures, what makes you shed tears or brings you laughter. I do not know the struggle against sin that lies within you, or all the signs of God's love in your life. I know nothing.

But Our Lady *does* know these things. Even if you forget all the words of this book, don't ever forget the answer Our Lady gave to Lucia's question about loneliness. "No, my daughter. Are you suffering a great deal? Don't lose heart. I will never forsake you. My Immaculate Heart will be your refuge and the way that will lead you to God."[117]

This answer is for *all of us*, no matter how we feel. This was Lucia's assurance for life, and it is ours as well. Our Lady reaffirms her presence in every little step of our way, and she assures us that she is our companion on our path to God.

---

[117]   Ibid., p. 177.

Our Lady understands this problem of loneliness in our time. She will never leave us! She is our refuge.

What does she mean here by a refuge? It is a shelter, a place where we feel secure, at peace, at home. That is what Our Lady wants to be to each one of us, a spiritual shelter, a home for our relationship with Jesus. The Portuguese episcopal conference, in the note for the Centennial of the Apparitions, put it this way: "For the Shepherd Children, the heart of the Lady was the sanctuary of their encounter with God."[118]

Mary's Intercession and Example

Two other aspects emerge from this promise Our Lady makes to Lucia: (1) Her intercession for us, and (2) her example.

Just as in Cana when she interceded for the bride and groom in need of her Son's help, today she intercedes for us. She can be our refuge because she still takes to Jesus what we are lacking.

The Second Vatican Council affirms Mary's continual role as an intercessor: "Taken up to heaven she did not lay aside this salvific duty, but by her constant intercession continued to bring us the gifts of eternal salvation."[119] Fatima is a call to trust in her "constant intercession."

Yet devotion to the Immaculate Heart of Mary is not simply expressed in the trust of someone who gives Mary all their worries and doubts; this devotion is also about

---

[118]   Conferência Episcopal Portuguesa, *Fátima sinal de esperança para o nosso tempo*, n. 10.
[119]   *Lumen Gentium*, no. 62.

imitation. It is about learning from her, the first and most perfect disciple, how to surrender to God.

Cardinal Ratzinger beautifully expresses the idea that to be devoted to Our Lady is to try to imitate her heart and to be willing to emulate her *fiat*. In his commentary on the third part of the Fatima secret, he says:

> In biblical language, the "heart" indicates the center of human life, the point where reason, will, temperament and sensitivity converge, where the person finds his unity and his interior orientation. According to Matthew 5:8, the "immaculate heart" is a heart which, with God's grace, has come to perfect interior unity and therefore "sees God". To be "devoted" to the Immaculate Heart of Mary means therefore to embrace this attitude of heart, which makes the *fiat*—"your will be done"—the defining center of one's whole life. It might be objected that we should not place a human being between ourselves and Christ. But then we remember that Paul did not hesitate to say to his communities: "imitate me" (*1 Cor* 4:16; *Phil* 3:17; *1 Th* 1:6; *2 Th* 3:7, 9). In the Apostle they could see concretely what it meant to follow Christ. But from whom might we better learn in every age than from the Mother of the Lord?[120]

So when Our Lady at Cana told the servants, "Do whatever he tells you" (Jn 2:5), she is describing her own behavior, showing us the secret of her own heart: she always did what

---

[120]   Joseph Ratzinger, *The Message of Fatima*, Congregation for the Doctrine of Faith, June 2000.

Jesus told her to do. As Cardinal Ratzinger said, she came to a perfect interior unity by living in accord with her original *fiat*, "your will be done, Lord!"

To be devoted to the Immaculate Heart of Mary means to come closer to this attitude of her heart so that our *fiat* will become the conforming axis of our existence. "Let it be done to me according to your will." That is what a true devotee of Mary learns to say to God, day by day. That is why Mary *is our way to God,* in the sense of being an example for us to become Christ-like. She was the first disciple, and she gives us the example so that all our will, our freedom, our memory, our affection, all our life revolves around the prayer, "let it be done according to your will."

The Triumph of the Immaculate Heart

Though we covered at length the July apparition in the last chapter, we return to it here briefly because there is yet another reference to the Immaculate Heart.

Our Lady said on July 13, 1917:

> You have seen hell where the souls of poor sinners go. To save them, God wishes to establish in the world devotion to my Immaculate Heart. If what I say to you is done, many souls will be saved and there will be peace. The war is going to end; but if people do not cease offending God, a worse one will break out. . . . To prevent this, I shall come to ask for the consecration of Russia to my Immaculate Heart, and the Communion of Reparation on the First Saturdays. If

my requests are heeded, Russia will be converted, and there will be peace; if not . . ."[121]

Isn't it amazing that Our Lord places within his mother's heart our path to peace and the salvation of many souls?

Cardinal Ratzinger marveled at this as well: "For one terrible moment, the children were given a vision of hell. They saw the fall of 'the souls of poor sinners.' And now they are told why they have been exposed to this moment: 'in order to save souls'— to show the way to salvation. To reach this goal, the way indicated —surprisingly for people from the Anglo-Saxon and German cultural world—is devotion to the Immaculate Heart of Mary."[122]

He goes on to discuss what Our Lady may have meant when she said, "my Immaculate Heart will triumph":

> I would like finally to mention another key expression of the "secret" which has become justly famous: "my Immaculate Heart will triumph." What does this mean? The Heart open to God, purified by contemplation of God, is stronger than guns and weapons of every kind. The fiat of Mary, the word of her heart, has changed the history of the world, because it brought the Savior into the world—because, thanks to her Yes, God could become man in our world and remains so for all time. The evil one has power in this world, as we see and experience continually; he has power because our freedom continually lets itself be led away from

---

[121] Lucia de Jesus, *Fatima in Lucia's own words*, p. 178-79.
[122] Joseph Ratzinger, *The Message of Fatima*, Congregation for the Doctrine of Faith, June 2000.

God. But since God himself took a human heart and has thus steered human freedom towards what is good, the freedom to choose evil no longer has the last word. From that time forth, the word that prevails is this: "In the world you will have tribulation, but take heart; I have overcome the world" (Jn 16:33). The message of Fatima invites us to trust in this promise.[123]

Yes, the Immaculate Heart of Mary will triumph when we—by fulfilling her requests of praying the Rosary, consecration to her Immaculate Heart, and reparation—open our hearts to the work of the Holy Spirit in such a way that he can form Christ in us! That is the true triumph of Mary, discrete and in silence, like it was all her life, like the triumph of Christ himself!

Jacinta, right before she left for the hospital where she would ultimately die, emphasized to Lucia the importance of devotion to the Immaculate Heart of Mary, saying:

> It will not be long now before I go to Heaven. You will remain here to make known that God wishes to establish in the world devotion to the Immaculate Heart of Mary. When you are to say this, don't go and hide. Tell everybody that God grants us graces through the Immaculate Heart of Mary; that people are to ask her for them; and that the Heart of Jesus wants the Immaculate Heart of Mary to be venerated at His side. Tell them also to pray to the Immaculate Heart of Mary for peace since God has entrusted it to her. If I could only put into the hearts of all, the fire that is

---

123   Ibid.

burning within my own heart, and that makes me love
the Hearts of Jesus and Mary so very much![124]

This little, sick, and holy girl reminds us that God has
entrusted peace to the Immaculate Heart of Mary. This
brings us to yet another dimension of Marian devotion that
emerges from Fatima.

All Is Within Her Heart

As we see in the Sacred Scriptures, Our Lady is described
as the "woman who kept everything in her heart" (Lk 2:19,
51). The first of these two verses refers to Mary's thoughts at
the time of the nativity, when Jesus was born in Bethlehem.
Our Lady did not fully understand what was unfolding, but
she "kept all these things, pondering them in her heart."
The other verse comes when she lost Jesus for three days
before finding him in Jerusalem speaking with the elders in
the Temple. When her Son replied with a somewhat curt
tone—"How is it that you sought me? Did you not know
that I must be in my Father's house?"—Mary again did not
understand but again "kept all these things in her heart."

She keeps in her heart everything that happens with Jesus
from Bethlehem to Jerusalem. In Bethlehem, where it all
starts. In Jerusalem, where it will all end. From the beginning to the end of Jesus's life, Mary kept everything in her
heart. Mary kept in her heart all the mysteries of the life of
Christ. This of course draws our minds to the Rosary, where
we meditate on all these mysteries.

---

[124]   Lucia de Jesus, *Fatima in Lucia's own words*, p. 132.

In the first meeting, when Lucia asked the lady her name, she did not answer. Instead, she told the children to pray the Rosary every day. They obeyed, month after month, until October 13, 1917, when she finally revealed her name, saying, "I am the Lady of the Rosary!"[125] Thus, we see an important connection between the praying of the Rosary and devotion to the Immaculate Heart of Mary. Through both, we enter into Our Lady's heart and discover the mysteries of Christ's life, which helps us come to know and love him all the more.

Standing Beneath the Cross

The nineteenth chapter of the Gospel of John is another text that seems evocative of Our Lady's appearance in Fatima. In that chapter, we see Mary as the woman at the foot of the cross. In the apparition to Sister Lucia in Tui, we see the Blessed Mother in that same location: "Beneath the right arm of the cross was Our Lady and in her hand was her Immaculate Heart. She appeared as Our Lady of Fatima, with her Immaculate Heart in her left hand, without sword or roses, but with a crown of thorns and flames."[126]

In this image, we see Our Lady who, with her Immaculate Heart, continues to accompany the Church on her way to the cross. This is why the pilgrims love her so much, because we know that today she stands by each of *our* crosses. It is the greatest consolation to have Mary's presence, of our mother's presence, close to us in our sufferings.

---

[125]   Ibid., p. 182.
[126]   Ibid., p. 197.

It is difficult whenever we feel like it is our turn to be on the cross. But we know that Our Lady, with her Immaculate Heart, is there too, helping us to be like Jesus while he was on his cross, living in obedience to the Father, offering ourselves as a gift of self for others.

A Woman of Light

In the description of the third part of the secret, Lucia describes Our Lady as full of light in such a way that the splendor that she radiates from her right hand annihilates the flames from the flaming sword.

As a matter of fact, when Lucia describes Our Lady, the most frequent (and forgotten) aspect is the light: "We beheld on a small holm oak, a Lady all dressed in white. She was more brilliant than the sun, and radiated a light more clear and intense."[127] "As she pronounced these last words—"the grace of God will be your comfort"—Our Lady opened her hands for the first time, communicating to us a light so intense that, as it streamed from her hands, its rays penetrated our hearts and the innermost depths of our souls, making us see ourselves in God, Who was that light, more clearly than we see ourselves in the best of mirrors."[128]

When we realize how often the word *light* or phrases like "woman more shining than the sun" are used in reference to Our Lady, how can we not think of chapter twelve of the book of Revelation? Here, in the "woman clothed with the sun", the Fathers of the Church saw an image of the Church, but also of Mary, the Mother of God. The apparitions at

---

[127]   Ibid., p. 174.
[128]   Ibid., p. 175.

Fatima again emphasize, through the omnipresence of this light, another aspect of Mary's role in the Scriptures.

Pope Francis beautifully explains this: "In Lucia's account, the three chosen children found themselves surrounded by God's light as it radiated from Our Lady. She enveloped them in the mantle of Light that God had given her. According to the belief and experience of many pilgrims, if not of all, Fatima is more than anything this mantle of Light that protects us, here as in almost no other place on earth."[129]

Just as the column of fire gave light to the chosen people in the Old Testament (see Ex 13:21) during their dark nights of pilgrimage through the desert, so the Virgin Mary, in her splendor, continues to guide the people of the New Covenant through the darkness of our nights, leading us securely to the promised land of the Heart of Jesus.

Treasures of the Immaculate Heart

The goal of this chapter has been to help you see the Immaculate Heart as a tangible companion in your spiritual path rather than some abstract spiritual concept or trivial style of art. Much was said, so let us conclude by way of a summary that condenses all these points down to simple takeaways.

- Sometimes it is difficult to know how we are meant to view the Blessed Mother and her role in salvation history. The Immaculate Heart gives us clarity on this.
- We are called first to trust in the power of the

---

[129]   Francis, Homily, Shrine of Fatima, May 13, 2017, Canonization of Francisco and Jacinta.

Immaculate Heart and only then will we understand it. If we wait to have all our questions answered, we will never have a devotion to it.

- The Angel of Peace spoke multiple times of the Heart of Mary, teaching us most of all that *it is in union with the Heart of Jesus* and that they have "designs of mercy" on all of us.

- Mary promises that the Immaculate Heart is our refuge, a place of sanctuary during times of suffering and a remedy to the loneliness and emptiness that so plagues our world.

- In coming into the refuge of her Immaculate Heart, she intercedes for us with her Son, as she did in Cana, and shows us how to imitate her, teaching us to live by her own words: "Let it be done according to your word."

- Scripture tells us that Mary "kept everything in her heart." This referred chiefly to the mysteries of her Son's life. By entering her Immaculate Heart, we enter into these mysteries and come to a greater wisdom of them.

- As the Fatima apparitions show us, Our Lady stands beneath her Son's cross with her Immaculate Heart in her hand. This assures us that she also stands with us when we are nailed to our own crosses of suffering.

- With yet another tie to the Mary from Scripture, we see her in Fatima as a woman bathed in light. It is the light of God which guides us on our journey home.

My friends, what treasures are hidden in the Immaculate Heart of Mary! I pray my simple words have made you aware of this treasure and inspire you towards a greater devotion to Mary's pure heart. I promise that if you make this devotion a central aspect of your spiritual life, she will purify your own heart so that you can "see God" (Mt 5:8).

That being said, we must learn what devotion to the Immaculate Heart looks like in practice. This chapter has attempted to show you the power associated with Our Lady's Immaculate Heart, but in the next chapters, we will show you the practical steps of living out this devotion.

CHAPTER 8

The Rosary

Three Requests

At Fatima, Our Lady makes three important requests of the children and of us. These three requests can be summed up in three words: (1) Rosary, (2) reparation, and (3) consecration. In this chapter, we will talk about the Rosary, leaving reparation and consecration for the next two.

All three of these requests have a double dimension to them: the mystical and the prophetic. Praying the Rosary, making acts of reparation, and the spiritual practice of consecration are all means of intensifying our relationship with God. This is the mystical nature of these requests. Yet they simultaneously express our solidarity with and our commitment to salvation history and so are prophetic as well. In other words, every time we pray the Rosary, not only does our union with God deepen, but we also grow in charity by helping to bring peace to the world and by saving souls. Clearly, if Our Lady's words are divorced from their mystical and prophetic dimensions, we cannot fully understand them or the full weight of what they are meant to convey to us.

A Brief History

This is not the place to present a full history of the Rosary, but a *brief* examination will serve us well.

In the early Church, monks and other religious prayed the 150 psalms, often using pebbles or seeds to mark them off. Many of the laity would have liked to increase their familiarity with the psalms, but this was a difficult practice for them to adopt because many could not read or were not educated enough to memorize them, not to mention Bibles were not commonly found in the home as they are now.

Therefore, in place of the 150 psalms, the people began praying "Our Lady's Psalter," the Hail Mary, also using various counting methods—including beads on a string—to keep track. Over time, other prayers were added and the stringed beads became more commonplace, turning it into the Rosary we know of today.

St. Dominic is said to have received a vision of Our Lady in the thirteenth century in which she gave him a rosary and asked him to preach about the Rosary to combat the Albigensian heresy. He and the Dominicans, the order he founded, are credited with popularizing the Rosary and spreading devotion to it.

Several centuries later, Pope Pius V credited the amazing Christian victory at the Battle of Lepanto (October 7, 1571) to the Rosary and Our Lady's intercession. To honor her help on that occasion and to commemorate the miraculous victory, he established the feast of Our Lady of Victory. His successor, Gregory XIII, then determined that this feast would be known as the "Solemnity of the Rosary."

These are just a few instances of how the Rosary came to be such an integral part of the Catholic faith. Countless pontifical documents have been written about the Rosary, encouraging the faithful to pray it and reflect on its spiritual and pastoral importance. The Rosary is one of the prayers most recommended by popes, from Pius V to Francis. For his part, John Paul II wrote an apostolic letter, *Rosarium Virginis Mariae* (*On the Rosary of the Virgin Mary*)[130] in which he underlined some theological elements about the Rosary, which we will highlight a little later.

A Christocentric Prayer

Years ago, many Catholic families gathered at the end of the day to pray the Rosary.

Though many do still today, this practice has waned in recent times.

This is most unfortunate! There is a reason Our Lady requested that the Rosary be prayed in all her apparitions at Fatima. She knows its importance.

Perhaps the gradual letting-go of this prayer—be it in our personal life or in the life of the family and the Church—is due to a lack of understanding of its profound meaning. If we only consider the Rosary's vocal dimension, we do not grasp its full efficacy. The Rosary is meant to be far more than just a vocal prayer. It is meant to configure us to Christ.

In his writings, Pope John Paul II makes this element of the Rosary explicit. While he recognizes that the body of the Rosary is made up of the vocal prayers—the Hail Mary, the

---

[130] John Paul II, Apostolic letter *Rosarium Virginis Mariae* (October 16, 2002).

Our Father, etc.—he understands that the soul of the Rosary is the mysteries of the life of Christ. The Rosary initiates us into these mysteries through Mary, with Mary, and like Mary.[131] In other words, we live these mysteries with and through her.

It is through the continual meditation on the Word of God, in the heart of Mary, that we can discern the origin of the Rosary. John Paul II expresses this insight in *Rosarium Virginis Mariae* when he says, "Mary lived with her eyes fixed on Christ, treasuring his every word: 'She kept all these things, pondering them in her heart' (Lk 2:19; cf. 2:51). The memories of Jesus, impressed upon her heart, were always with her, leading her to reflect on the various moments of her life at her Son's side. In a way those memories were to be the 'rosary' which she recited uninterruptedly throughout her earthly life."[132]

To pray the Rosary with Mary is to contemplate the mysteries of Christ that she kept in her heart. If we understand that we are meditating on the mysteries of Jesus through the eyes of Mary, it changes our approach to the Rosary. All of us love to reminisce about those we love, and Mary is no different. No one loved Jesus more than Mary, and she wants to share this powerful love with us by helping us to contemplate the mysteries of his life.

Some people have trouble with the repetitive nature of the Rosary. I used to be one of those people until I began to understand why the repetition is important. The repetition allows the mysteries to move from the mind to the heart. It

---

[131]   See Ibid., nos. 10, 12, 13.
[132]   Ibid., no. 38.

brings a powerful rhythm to our prayers, allowing the soul to take flight. You might say it allows our hearts to beat in harmony with the rhythm of Mary's heart.

The Rosary is, of course, a Marian prayer, a prayer of praise to the Mother of God. The Rosary is also the fulfilment of Mary's words in her *Magnificat* (Lk 1:46–55), when she said to her cousin Elizabeth, "all generations will call me blessed." When we pray the Rosary, we fulfil her prophecy and also count ourselves among those generations who call Mary blessed.

Clearly, there is no question that Our Lady is, at every turn, profoundly connected to the Rosary, but at its core, the Rosary is *a Christocentric prayer*. Mary would not be blessed if she had not given her great *fiat*, had not agreed, to God's request to become the mother of his Son, if she had not agreed to be overshadowed by the power of the Holy Spirit, and if she had not agreed to carry, bear, and raise the Messiah. The whole purpose of the Rosary is to deepen our bond with Jesus through Mary. Pope John Paul II said the Rosary is "a compendium of the Gospel,"[133] not only because its prayers are taken from the New Testament, but also because the joyful, sorrowful, and glorious mysteries refer to many of the most important moments in Christ's life.

However, John Paul II, who was himself very devoted to the Rosary, noticed that although these mysteries cover Christ's birth and his early life, his passion and death, his resurrection and the events that happened shortly thereafter, most of the events of Christ's ministry were not covered. To remedy this situation, in 2002, he introduced the Luminous

---

[133]   Ibid., no. 18.

Mysteries so that the mysteries of the Rosary would be a summary of Christ's *whole* life. Significantly, the Luminous Mysteries are sometimes called the Mysteries of Light, which resonates with the emphasis placed on light in the apparitions of Fatima. These mysteries of light, introduced by John Paul II, include Christ's baptism in the Jordan by John the Baptist, the beginning of Christ's public ministry by working the miracle at the wedding feast of Cana, the proclamation of the kingdom, his transfiguration on Mount Tabor, and his institution of the Eucharist at the Last Supper. Clearly his motivation for adding this fourth set of mysteries stemmed from his recognition of the total Christological nature of the prayer.

However, praying the Rosary is not only contemplating the mysteries of the life of Jesus through the eyes of Mary. It also invites us to contemplate our own lives through the eyes of Jesus and Mary. As we pray, we consider the mysteries of our daily lives, both its joys and its sorrows, in relation to the mysteries of Jesus's life. By doing this, we gain a certain spiritual capacity to read the events of our lives in the light of Jesus's life, and we commit to Mary's heart the things that matter most to us, knowing that her maternal eyes will watch over them.

If it is true that "only in the mystery of the incarnate Word does the mystery of man take on light,"[134] then the Rosary is a privileged way for us to know more deeply our own mystery in the light of God's gaze. This knowledge deepens our understanding of life, helps us to accept and better navigate some of its chaos, and gives us a sense of peace in this

---

[134]   Second Vatican Council, *Gaudium et Spes* (1965), no. 22.

turbulent world, because by praying a Christocentric prayer each day, we begin to live a Christocentric life.

A Prayer for the Church

The ecclesial dimension of the Rosary is another aspect of this prayer that is very important to reflect upon. This prayer holds an important place in the life of the Church. Allow me to give a personal story to demonstrate this.

In 2013, after being nominated postulator for the cause of the shepherd children, I was sent to Rome for three months, from January through March. It was a difficult trip because I had to leave my religious community for the first time and be totally by myself.

On February 11, an event of great importance broke the rhythm of my long hours of research and other laborious tasks concerning the cause. On that day, something unimaginable happened: Pope Benedict XVI resigned. I quickly realized I was living through a unique time in history. From the vantage point of my residence in the Portuguese College just behind the Vatican, I was an eyewitness at the epicenter of this nearly unprecedented event in the life of the Church.

On February 28, at 8:00 p.m., when *sede vacante* would begin, I had what I thought would be a unique and brilliant idea. I planned to walk over to Saint Peter's Square to pray for the Church. When I arrived, I was surprised to find that thousands of people had the very *same* brilliant idea! The piazza was full of people, despite its being a cold, wet night.

I decided to find a group I could pray with and so began traversing the square. The first group I saw was praying in English, which I could speak relatively well, but it was too big a group and I could not hear well enough. I departed for another group. This one was speaking Frénch . . . alas, I do not speak French! But before I walked away, I heard . . . *Je vous salue, Marie pleine de grâce* . . . I realized they were praying the Rosary and decided to stay. The group began to grow and the square concentrated there, bringing people from other nationalities in. The first part of the Hail Mary was in French, but the second part was in Portuguese, and then also in Spanish and in Italian, and in Polish, and so on, even in languages I did not recognize.

After some time, I stopped and marveled at the moment. We all knew what we were praying, we all understood each other, despite the Babel-like conditions. We all knew how and why we were praying, with Our Lady, for the Holy Spirit to come down upon the Church at this delicate moment in her history.

What moment does this remind you of?

Pentecost!

At the birth of the Church, when thousands of people from all around the globe heard each of the apostles speaking in their own languages, Mary was humbly present. As John Paul II has said, "The rosary is the prayer that Mary prays along with us, just as she prayed with the Apostles in the Upper-Room. . . . Nonetheless, let us not forget that the rosary is our prayer with Mary and it is the prayer of Mary with us, with the successors of the Apostles, who formed the new People of Israel, the new People of God."[135]

This personal experience of praying the Rosary in communion with thousands of others showed that, in some

---

[135]   John Paul II, Homily, Pompei-Italy, October 21, 1979.

circumstances, there is no other prayer like the Rosary to build up the Church, to make from the holy people of God a community in prayer, a living body praying together.

Becoming Christlike

Another important aspect of the Rosary is the way it leads us along the path to holiness.

As a novice, I remember that "all" I wanted was to become a saint. It had been difficult for me to leave my family and my future career in order to enter convent life, so I vowed to make my time "worth it" by becoming a saint.

When I turned to the Scriptures to learn what it meant to be a saint, I quickly discovered that keeping the commandments was not enough. After all, look what Christ told the rich young man (see Lk 18:18–30). It obviously was also not enough simply to follow Christ, for even Peter followed from a distance both before and after betraying him (see Lk 22:54–62).

When I eventually turned to the letters of St. Paul, he gave me the answer: "My little children, with whom I am again in travail until Christ be formed in you!" (Gal 4:19). So, it was necessary that Christ *was formed* in me. Paul goes on to advise that it is essential to have "the same feelings as Christ" (cf. Phil 2:4). I understood this was sanctity.

Very soon I realized that my smallest efforts to "become like Christ" seemed to be in vain. The same faults, the same limitations, the same sins that I so often suffer from cropped up again and again. I became discouraged. It was the beginning of a vocational crisis for me. If I was not going to become a saint, what was the point of the religious life?

In those days, I understood nothing of the spiritual life, but I did the best I could. I sought guidance from my superior and from my spiritual director. But they could not help me. No one could. The root of the problem was the relationship between the will of God, the grace of God, and my own will.

Then on October 16, 2002, I read *Rosarium Virginis Mariae* (*The Rosary of the Virgin Mary*). One of John Paul's reflections in that apostolic letter brought me great clarity: "The Rosary mystically transports us to Mary's side as she is busy watching over the human growth of Christ in the home of Nazareth. This enables her to train us and to mold us with the same care, until Christ is 'fully formed' in us (cf. Gal 4:19)."[136]

He was quoting the exact same passage from St. Paul's letters that had led to my crisis! Except John Paul was telling me that it would be Our Lady who would do the "work" of molding me and my heart, until Christ—not her, but her Son—would be fully formed in me.

So I prayed, "Blessed Mother, the Rosary I can pray! But you have to do the rest! And I know that along with the Holy Spirit, Jesus's features will be carved in my soul, slowly, at the pace of my daily Rosary." This is the deepest power of the Rosary: to mold us until we become a living memory of Christ, to make us Christ-like. This is what it is to be a saint—a vocation to which we are all called!

---

[136] John Paul II, *Rosarium Virginis Mariae*, no. 15.

The Prophetic Dimension of the Rosary

Thus far, we have discussed the mystical dimension of the Rosary, but let's now turn to its prophetic dimension.

Our Lady teaches us in Fatima that prayer is a fundamental requirement for peace and that the Rosary is specifically intended to promote peace—both for the individual and for the world.

In 1917, when the apparitions first occurred, World War I was raging. The shepherd children knew nothing about Russia, but they knew exactly what war meant. In response to the violence, Our Lady was unconditional in her desires: "I want you to come here on the thirteenth of next month, to continue to pray the Rosary every day in honor of Our Lady of the Rosary, in order to obtain peace for the world and the end of the war, because only she can help you."[137]

The disproportion between the simplicity of what is being asked with the immensity of graces that we are promised may seem strange to our way of seeing things. How can we help end a war simply by praying the Rosary every day?

This brings to mind the scene of Naaman the Syrian, disappointed because the prophet Elisha, in order to cure him, merely asked him to bathe seven times in the Jordan River (see 2 Kgs 5). For him, who had travelled from so far, he who was such an important man, full of himself and of his plans, to see his cure as merely "bathing" in a foreign river? It was unthinkable. Yet his servants implored him to listen and obey, saying, "My father, if the prophet had commanded you to do some great thing, would you not have done it?

---

[137]   Lucia de Jesus, *Fatima in Lucia's own words*, vol. 1, 22.ª ed. (Fátima: Fundação Francisco e Jacinta Marto, 2018), p. 178.

How much rather, then, when he says to you, 'Wash, and be clean!'" (2 Kgs 5:13).

Likewise, Our Lady asks us to do something very simple and accessible. All it requires is obedience in faith and love. So why don't we do it? Like Naaman, do we have a hard time believing that something so simple could produce such amazing results? Or that obedience to God is more efficacious than our own plans?

For many of us, we simply lack the faith to believe that Our Lady will do what she promises or that such wonderful results could occur simply as a result of our obedience. There is no question that lack of faith and lack of trust in the means God suggests often hold us back. Most of us always want *our* will to be done rather than *his*. This is, of course, obvious when we commit sins through following our own will. But even when we strive to do good, we typically want to do it on our own timetable and by the means we deem the worthiest rather than by simply doing what God asks us to do.

To want what God wants, this is the secret to holiness. This is the expression of a humble heart which attracts the gaze of God and the Lord of Peace upon us. Even if we do not love the Rosary, even if we do not understand its worth, even if we find it boring, but we pray it simply because Our Lady asks us to, we will already be doing everything asked of us by heaven.

Pray the Rosary Everyday

In one of my visits to Sister Lucia, a gentleman from the United States went with me. He presented her with some requests, some intentions for which he asked her to pray. She said, "Yes, I will pray. But you, too, please, pray the rosary every day."

She said this with such conviction that I couldn't help thinking, *this woman knows more than I do. If she insists on the praying of the Rosary, she might have a reason.* I will never forget that moment.

As I noted earlier, if you wait until you feel you understand the Rosary before starting to pray it, you will neither pray it nor understand it. We need to learn from St. Francisco Marto's response when Our Lady told him that he needed to pray many rosaries in order to go to heaven: "Oh, my dear Lady! I'll say as many rosaries as you want!"[138] And then, yes, we will understand it.

May the Rosary be for each of us our beloved prayer where our hearts meet Mary's heart and are transformed to beat in union with the heart of Christ. When we hold the Rosary in our hands, we hold one of the greatest secrets of Fatima; we hold at our fingertips the light that shines forth to the world from Fatima.

---

[138]   Lucia de Jesus, *Fatima in Lucia's own words*, p. 143.

CHAPTER 9

Understanding Reparation

Finding the Proper Perspective

Much has been said and written about reparation and consecration, two important aspects of the Fatima message, and not always with great clarity. It is important to understand the nature of both reparation and consecration in light of the Sacred Scriptures and the paschal mystery of Jesus Christ. This is how we gain the proper perspective for all things in life, and so of course this is how it is for all the requests of the Mother of God.

Two things will be carried over from the last chapter on the Rosary. First, we are making a Christological reading of these requests. They are seen not as means to put Mary at the center of our lives and humanity but Christ *through* Mary. Two, we see the continued presence of the two dimensions ever-present in Fatima: mystical and prophetic. In consecration, we see the mystical, deepening our union with Christ, and in reparation, we participate in the history of salvation, cooperating with God's saving work and bringing peace to the world. So both reparation and consecration increase our relationship with God, our intimacy with God, and also show Our Lord that we are committed to participating in the history of salvation.

Reparation in the Apparitions

We will focus on consecration in the next chapter. For now, let us turn to reparation.

Right from the first cycle of apparitions in 1916, the angel speaks about reparation. Specifically, in the second apparition, he says, "Make of everything you can a sacrifice, and offer it to God as an act of reparation for the sins by which He is offended, and in supplication for the conversion of sinners."[139]

He refers again to reparation in the third apparition, when the angel taught them the prayer to the Most Holy Trinity: ". . . present in all the tabernacles of the world, in reparation for the outrages, sacrileges and indifference with which He Himself is offended . . ."[140]

After giving Communion to the shepherd children, although he did not explicitly use the word, the angel referred to the act of reparation: "Take and drink the Body and Blood of Jesus Christ, horribly outraged by ungrateful men. Repair their crimes and console your God."[141]

In the May apparition, Our Lady also mentions reparation. Posing one of the fundamental questions in the history of Fatima, she asks the children, "Are you willing to

---

[139]   Lucia de Jesus, *Fatima in Lucia's own words*, vol. 1, 22.ª ed. (Fátima: Fundação Francisco e Jacinta Marto, 2018), p. 171.

[140]   Ibid., p. 172.

[141]   Ibid..

offer yourselves to God and bear all the sufferings He wills to send you, as an act of reparation for the sins by which He is offended, and of supplication for the conversion of sinners?"[142]

In her words, Our Lady makes clear that, in this case, reparation implies an offering of one's whole life.

After seeing the heart encircled by thorns in the June apparition, Lucia herself evokes reparation as the key to understanding the vision: "We understood that this was the Immaculate Heart of Mary, outraged by the sins of humanity and seeking reparation."[143]

In the July apparition, Our Lady once again returned to the subject of reparation when she gave the shepherd children a prayer to pray whenever they made sacrifices: "O Jesus, it is for love of You, for the conversion of sinners, and in reparation for the sins committed against the Immaculate Heart of Mary."[144]

And right after the vision of hell, in the second part of the secret, Our Lady says, "To prevent this . . . I shall come to ask for the consecration of Russia to my Immaculate Heart and the communion of reparation on the First Saturdays."[145]

Quite clearly, the theme of reparation consistently and repeatedly runs through the entire message of Fatima.

---

[142]   Ibid., p. 175.
[143]   Ibid., p. 177.
[144]   Ibid., p. 178.
[145]   Ibid., p. 179.

What Is Reparation?

What is reparation? What exactly does it mean? Why did Our Lady of Fatima and the angel ask the children (and us) to make reparation, and why did she consider this so important?

Etymologically, the word *reparation* means "to restore," "to rebuild," or "to renew."

In the context of the Fatima apparitions, reparation refers to repairing and rebuilding but also consoling. These two dimensions—to restore/rebuild and to console—are present in an expression used by the angel: "Repair their crimes and console your God." Nevertheless, this was not the only apparition where the request of reparation was made, as we saw.

Trying to answer these questions, we will consider the challenges given by the Sacred Scriptures and the light given by the paschal mystery of Jesus. Finally, we will look at what Our Lady specifically requested we do to make reparation, focusing on the First Saturday Devotion and how to fulfill her request.

A Book of Questions

I have always thought of the Bible as a book of questions. It is more than this, obviously, but what do I mean by this?

At the very beginning, in Genesis, God asks two important questions: "Where are you?" and, "Where is your brother?" The first he asks Adam and Eve after they have eaten of the forbidden tree and are hiding from him. The second is directed to Cain after he has killed his brother, Able.

These questions can be addressed to us as well. God is asking about our place in history and the meaning of our lives. The first question highlights the importance of our relationship with God, the necessity of our not hiding from him, and our need to develop a loving relationship with him. The second focuses on the degree to which we are responsible to help our "brother" and calls to mind our responsibility for our brothers and sisters, for the history of salvation, and for peace in the world.

In Fatima, the Virgin Mother invites us to answer these questions with consecration and reparation, but we will leave the first for the next chapter.

The Vertical and Horizontal Dimensions of Reparation

Christ's cross helps us to understand reparation because "reparation is only understood within the framework of salvation, perceived as the process initiated by God, who comes down to man in history, to lead him to the fullness of life in communion with Him." [146] The nature of reparation is to be a witness to the excess of God's love towards humanity, overflowing with the gift of life for others, as Jesus did. The fundamental characteristic of this model of reparation is to be moved by love. It is the loving heart that we wish to repair, and we repair it with love.[147].

---

[146]   Nurya Martínez-Gayol, *Los excesos del amor: figuras femininas de reparación en la Edad Media* (siglos XI-XIV) (Madrid: San Pablo, 2012), p. 343.

[147]   Cf. Ibid., p. 347.

The vertical dimension, represented by the stem of the cross, symbolizes our relationship with God, while the horizontal dimension, represented by the cross beam, represents our relationship to others.

Let us begin with the horizontal arm, trying to understand reparation from the perspective of our call to participate in the salvific mystery on behalf of others. This means we reflect on reparation as an act of love, of solidarity in the Trinitarian love for the salvation of the world.[148] This is correctly understood only by referring constantly to the paschal mystery, to the mystery of the passion, death, and resurrection of Jesus.

Reading the first chapters of Genesis, we realize that until sin entered the world, we were in perfect harmony with ourselves, with God, and with the world around us. But then sin enters and all becomes broken. Adam and Eve are expelled from paradise, severing their relationship with God, and what follows is conflict between human beings, seen through the story of Cain and Able, and even suffering among creation, seen in the flood at the time of Noah. With sin, the three basic dimensions of humanity are broken. And this goes on unrelentingly, with no solution, until the passion, death, and resurrection of Jesus, who restores these three relationships.

After Jesus's paschal mystery, he restored our relationship with God, and we became his children once more. Then,

---

[148]   António Marto, *Fátima: uma luz sobre a história do mundo*, in COUTINHO, Vítor (coord.). *Mensagem de Esperança para o mundo: Acontecimento e significado de Fátima* (Fátima: Santuário de Fátima, 2012), p. 41.

he restored our relationship with one another, and truly we became brothers and sisters, including Jesus's.

In one moment, Jesus said to his apostles, "No longer do I call you servants . . . but I have called you friends" (Jn 15:15). Then after his paschal mystery, they are no longer only friends, but brothers: "Do not be afraid. Go and tell my brethren to go to Galilee, and there they will see me" (Mt 28:10).

Pope Francis explained this dynamic very clearly:

> The root of all evil, as we know, is sin, which from its first appearance has disrupted our communion with God, with others and with creation itself. This rupture of communion with God likewise undermines our harmonious relationship with the environment in which we are called to live, so that the garden has become a wilderness (cf. *Gen* 3:17–18). Creation urgently needs the revelation of the children of God, who have been made "a new creation." The path to Easter demands that we renew our faces and hearts as Christians through repentance, conversion and forgiveness, so as to live fully the abundant grace of the paschal mystery. . . . It invites Christians to embody the paschal mystery more deeply and concretely in their personal, family and social lives. Let us leave behind our selfishness and self-absorption, and turn to Jesus' Paschal Mystery. Let us stand beside our brothers and sisters in need, sharing our spiritual and material goods with them. In this way, by concretely welcoming Christ's

victory over sin and death into our lives, we will also radiate its transforming power to all of creation.[149]

However, as Francis notes, "In this world, the harmony generated by redemption is constantly threatened by the negative power of sin and death."[150]

As Scripture tells us, this negative power actually affects all of creation, for after the fall, all creation "groaned." For this reason, the pope emphasizes that "Creation [itself] urgently needs to partake of the renewal of the children of God, who have been made a new creation." Through his paschal mystery, Jesus "makes all things new" (Rv 21:5). The very creation partakes of the paschal mystery by opening up a new heaven and a new earth.

And interestingly, in Fatima, we can even perceive this cosmic dimension, as one theologian pointed out: "It is a persistent theme (reparation) where the cosmic participation of the mystery is represented by the miracle of the sun, which means that peace with God and reparation entail, in its rewarding dynamics, not only humanity but also nature and its cosmic dimension."[151]

We are all invited to cooperate in this work of salvation by our reparation, which is our cooperation in the act of restoring this dynamic that evil causes in the world.

Our Lady invites each of us, through reparation, to participate in this renewal. In contrast with the post-modern

---

[149] Pope Francis, Message of his holiness for Lent, 2019.
[150] Ibid.
[151] José Jacinto Farias, O Coração de Maria e a mística da reparação, *Didaskalia* (Lisboa: Universidade Católica Editora, 47:1, 2017), p. 219.

world which exalts individuality and the self over everything else, Our Lady urges us to step *out of ourselves,* to think of others, to feel responsible for them.

Now let us consider the vertical dimension of reparation, our relationship with God and our desire to console him.

This presents a bit of a theological challenge. Does God suffer? *Can* he suffer?

Hans Urs von Balthasar says that "God suffers with us and much more than we do; and will not cease to suffer while there is suffering in the world."[152] God does not suffer because of the weakness of his nature but because of the strength of his love.[153]

It is love that explains reparation. Love is what heals all wounds. Like Lucia explained, "I myself think that what purifies us is love, the fire of divine Love, communicated by God to souls."[154]

But how can we console God? Pope Benedict XVI explained this well: "The Latin word *con-solatio,* 'consolation,' expresses this beautifully. It suggests *being with* the other in his solitude, so that it ceases to be solitude."[155]

---

[152] H. U. von Balthasar, *Theodramatik IV Das Endspiel* (Einsiedeln 1983), 239. Quoted by João António Pinheiro Teixeira, Um coração em trespasse na Cruz, *Didaskalia* (Lisboa: Universidade Católica Editora, 47:1, 2017), p. 158.

[153] Cf. João António Pinheiro Teixeira, Um coração em trespasse na Cruz, *Didaskalia* (Lisboa: Universidade Católica Editora, 47:1, 2017), p. 159.

[154] Lucia de Jesus, *The message of Fatima: how I see the Message in the course of time and in the light of events* (Fátima: Carmelo de Coimbra; Secretariado dos Pastorinhos, 2006), p. 34.

[155] Pope Bededict XVI, Encyclical *Spe Salvi* (2007), no. 38.

So we console God by our very companionship with him. This was one of the most important characteristics of Francisco's spirituality, who, after the words of the angel "console your God," could not think about anything else but keeping a sad Jesus company. To make reparation, then, is to console God and the Immaculate Heart of Mary by spending time with them.

If this seems abstract, perhaps an analogy will help. Imagine a wealthy mother with two daughters. The first daughter goes to the mother every day to ask for something: "I need this." "I need that." The mother gives this daughter what she asks for because the mother is wealthy and she wants to make her child happy. The second daughter also goes to see her mother every day, but rather than constantly asking for things, this daughter visits her mother to do things for her, to keep her company, to ask her what she would like. Which of these daughters seems to love her mother more? Obviously, the second daughter.

In our relationship with God, it is always a good idea to ask, "Are we more like the first or second daughter?" If you are anything like me, it is the first daughter!

It is good to ask Jesus for what we need. After all, he told us to: "Ask, and it will be given you; seek, and you will find; knock, and it will be opened to you" (Mt 7:7). But if our relationship with Jesus is only based on asking for things, this is not yet a pure love. In such cases, there is a great risk that we look for him only to receive his gifts and not because we love him, like the bride who cherishes her diamond ring, but not so much the man who gave it to her.

In a relationship, if someone is always looking for what the other person can give, this is not love. A relationship founded on true love is an exchange of hearts, with both parties making the donation of self for the good of the other. Love ends where one focuses mainly or exclusively on oneself.

Reparation is a remedy for this selfishness. It is a great lesson in and opportunity for us to learn how to love God above all things, even above our own often very worthwhile intentions. What a consolation to God it must be to see us come to him every day not only to ask but also to give, to give him our time and our love.

The Greatest Commandment

Having considered these two dimensions of reparation—the vertical and the horizontal—we can understand why reparation is all about love.

You may recall that when asked what the greatest commandment is, Jesus replied, "You shall love the Lord your God with all your heart, and with all your soul, and with all your mind. This is the great and first commandment. And a second is like it, You shall love your neighbor as yourself. On these two commandments depend all the law and the prophets" (Mt 22:37–40).

By consoling God, by praying to give ourselves to him rather than making requests, we show that we love him above all things. By cooperating in the paschal mystery through reparation, we show that we love our brothers and sisters as ourselves. By making reparation, we cooperate, to the best of our ability, in God's plans for the history of salvation. Thus, reparation helps us put these two greatest commandments of our Lord into action.

So what does all this mean?

It means that each time I make an act of reparation, I am collaborating with Christ in repairing our broken relationships with God, with our fellow human beings, and with creation.

Each time I do the First Saturdays, or pray a Rosary and offer sacrifices in reparation, I am doing it in union with the paschal mystery, in union with *the* moment of reparation in our history of salvation. We are accepting Christ's and Mary's invitation to go more deeply into the paschal mystery in our personal lives.

This helps us see that reparation—and the First Saturdays Devotion—is much greater than just a pious devotion. Antonio Marto, the cardinal of Fatima, summarizes it as follows:

> Reparation is, first of all, another way of saying the mystery of redemption. It is God who offers reparation for the sin of the world, in Jesus. In His surrender until the end, Jesus did everything until death to repair, that is, to renew man's heart, reestablish his communion with God, reconcile men with God, overcome the force of sin in the world. It is God Himself who with His love enters in the sufferings of history not only to create a balance between the weight of evil and good, but for an overabundance of grace, a boost of love stronger than the abundance of evil. This "reparation" is within the logic of love and reconciliation,

it is an expression of solidarity in the Trinitarian love for the salvation of the world.[156]

You at Least . . .

Now that we understand the nature of reparation and how profound it is, we must ask ourselves if we are willing to make this a part of our spiritual lives. Let me share a story from my own life that gave me great clarity in answering this call of reparation.

Our Lord and Our Lady asked for the reparation of the First Saturday in the apparition in Pontevedra, Spain, on December 10, 1925. The most holy Virgin appeared to Sister Lucia, and by her side, elevated on a luminous cloud, was a child. The most holy Virgin rested her hand on Lucia's shoulder, and as Our Lady did so, she showed her a heart encircled by thorns, which she was holding in her other hand. At the same time, the Child said, "Have compassion on the Heart of your most holy Mother, covered with thorns, with which ungrateful men pierce it at every moment, and there is no one to make an act of reparation to remove them."

Then the most holy Virgin said, "Look, my daughter, at my Heart, surrounded with thorns with which ungrateful men pierce me every moment by their blasphemies and ingratitude. You at least try to console me and say that I promise to assist at the hour of death, with the graces necessary for salvation, all those who, on the first Saturday of

---

[156]   António Marto, *Fátima: uma luz sobre a história do mundo*, in COUTINHO, Vítor (coord.)., *Mensagem de Esperança para o mundo: Acontecimento e significado de Fátima* (Fátima: Santuário de Fátima, 2012), p. 41-43.

five consecutive months, shall confess, receive Holy Communion, recite five decades of the Rosary, and keep me company for fifteen minutes while meditating on the fifteen mysteries of the Rosary, with the intention of making reparation to me."[157]

So Our Lady comes with her Immaculate Heart in her hand, covered with thorns to symbolize her suffering, which results from her children's tearing themselves away from God. But Jesus also comes, and he is the first to speak. The core of this First Saturday devotion is making reparation to the Immaculate Heart of Mary, but God wants to ensure us that this devotion is God's will. This is why the Holy Infant comes as well.

Jesus asks Lucia to "have compassion on the heart of your mother." Have compassion . . . in other words, think about her with love. Accompany her in her suffering. Furthermore, Jesus underlines that Our Lady is Lucia's mother: "*your* mother!" He wants us to be aware of Mary's spiritual maternity.

Then, continuing, he laments, "and there is no one to make an act of reparation to remove them." According to Jesus's request, making reparation is, symbolically, like removing the thorns from her heart.

Finally, Our Lady speaks, and the first sentence is more or less a repetition of Our Lord's words, stressing a filial relationship: "Look, *my daughter* . . ." She is echoing her Son and emphasizing that she is our mother.

---

[157]   Lucia de Jesus, *Fatima in Lucia's own words*, p. 194.

After she highlights the same thorns stuck in her heart that her Son referred to, she says, "You at least try to console me." This phrase "*you at least*" changed my life.

When I was discerning my religious vocation, I had a vocational crisis. (I told you I had some of them!) As a result of certain events from my youth, I considered not following the call from God to the religious life, even though I was quite sure he was calling me to that life. I was struggling so much that I increased my prayer life.

As I mentioned in the first chapter, after the death of my father, my mother had moved to Porto, and along with her friend Maria Clara and the sisters of Aliança de Santa Maria, we started to do the First Saturday Devotion. Just to refresh my memory about the text concerning this devotion, I decided to look at *Fatima in Lucia's Own Words*. When I read the phrase, "you at least try to console me," my heart stopped! I almost felt as if Our Lady was telling me, "You at least, Angela, try to be faithful to Jesus's call."

At that moment, I realized that nobody could replace me in my vocation, just as nobody can replace you in yours. Each of us must take up the mantle of reparation, individually. Will you answer when Our Lady asks, "You at least . . ."? Will you console her and your God?

Fulfilling the First Saturday Devotion

You may say, after reading all this about reparation, "Yes, Sister, I want to make reparation. I want to console my God and his mother!" But you may then ask, "How exactly do I answer this call?"

Here is what Our Lord and Our Lady ask us to do specifically to fulfill the request of reparation through the First Saturday Devotion.

On the first Saturday of five consecutive months, we should:

1. **Pray five decades of the Rosary.** This can be any set of mysteries we like, but typically on Saturday we are to pray the Joyful Mysteries.

2. **Keep Our Lady company for fifteen minutes while meditating on the mysteries of the Rosary.** Our Lady is asking for meditation on the Sacred Scriptures. This is the first time in the history of apparitions that Our Lady asks for meditation on the Gospels. She knows quite well that without meditation on the Gospel, people cannot become Christ-like.

3. **Go to confession.** It is best to go on that Saturday, but in a subsequent apparition of the Child Jesus, he granted the possibility of confessing at some other time during the month, so long as Communion was taken in a state of grace and people would not forget to express their intention of reparation.

4. **Receive Holy Communion.** And, of course, all these requirements are fulfilled by going to Mass and receiving Communion. As Cardinal Antonio Marto explained, "It is not surprising that the dynamism of reparation has its privileged moment in the Eucharistic participation and communion, where we are immersed in a wave of tributary Love,

in its vertical movement from God to Man and in its
horizontal movement of communion and circulation
of love among all, in favor of each other."[158]

Some people wonder about a "technicality" involving the
fulfillment of this last request; namely, must we attend a Saturday *morning* Mass or can we simply attend the vigil that
evening, which satisfies our Sunday obligation? My answer
to them is that Our Lady simply asked for Communion on
that first Saturday of the month. If we have the time, we
can go in the morning and go again for our Sunday obligation the next day. However, if life's circumstances prevent
this, the devotion can be lived and completed by attending the Saturday vigil Mass with the intention of satisfying
Our Lady's requests (and, of course, by fulfilling the other
requests as well).

After she made these requests, Our Lady made a "promise"
to assist each soul who fulfilled them with all the graces necessary for eternal salvation. After declaring that her Immaculate Heart is in this life our refuge and the way leading us
to God, she assures us that it will also be our safe shelter at
the moment of death. The love of the hearts of Jesus and
Mary for us expresses itself in this infinitely great promise—
to grant her company and assistance with all graces needed
for salvation to all who practice, in a spirit of reparation, the
First Saturday Devotion.

---

[158]   António Marto, *Fátima: uma luz sobre a história do mundo*, in
COUTINHO, Vítor (coord.), *Mensagem de Esperança para o
mundo: Acontecimento e significado de Fátima* (Fátima: Santuário
de Fátima, 2012), p. 43.

A curious reader might wonder why it is *five* first Saturdays and not some other number. Is there any significance to five?

When this question was posed to Sister Lucia, she answered, in a letter, by relaying words from Our Lord: "My daughter the reason is very simple: There are five types of offenses and blasphemies made against the Immaculate Heart of Mary: First, the blasphemies against the Immaculate Conception. Second, against her virginity. Third, against her divine maternity, refusing at the same time to accept her as the mother of all mankind. Fourth, those who try publicly to instill in children's hearts indifference, contempt and even hate against this Immaculate Mother. Fifth, those who insult her directly in her sacred images."[159]

Our Lord here gives us the reason for the specific number associated with the devotion. Five Saturdays consoling her with our love!

The First Saturdays Devotion was approved by Bishop José Alves Correia da Silva on September 13, 1939, and thousands upon thousands of devout souls have practiced it ever since. I implore you, dear reader, to consider completing this devotion. I know it is difficult with the chaos of our lives, but the spiritual fruit it will bear is unimaginable, and as we have learned, it will console God and his holy mother, and we will cooperate in the history of salvation of your brothers and sisters. And when we deeply understand how much our love grows with this devotion, five months will not be enough!

---

[159]   Letter from Sr. Lucia to Fr. Gonçalves, 12 June 1930.

CHAPTER 10

Understanding Consecration

"Where Are You?"

In the last chapter, we discussed a question God posed to Adam and Eve shortly after they disobeyed him and were hiding from him. He asked, "Where are you?" God poses this same question to us, and by answering it, we, too, are challenged to think about the meaning of our lives.

In Fatima, we are given a means to answer this question. The answer is *consecration*. By our consecration to Our Lord through the Immaculate Heart of Mary, we tell Our Lord exactly where we are: we are in the womb of the Blessed Mother, we are in the Church, we belong to the mystical Body of Christ, with the heart of Mary.

So let us talk now about this important aspect of the Fatima message.

Consecration in the Apparitions

Our Lady spoke of consecration to her Immaculate Heart twice in the story of Fatima: (1) In the apparition of July and (2) the apparition of Tui.

On July 13, 1917, she said:

> To prevent this, I shall come to ask for the conse-
> cration of Russia to my Immaculate Heart, and the
> Communion of Reparation on the First Saturdays. If
> my requests are heeded, Russia will be converted, and
> there will be peace; if not, she will spread her errors
> throughout the world, causing wars and persecutions
> of the Church. The good will be martyred, the Holy
> Father will have much to suffer, various nations will
> be annihilated. In the end, my Immaculate Heart will
> triumph. The Holy Father will consecrate Russia to
> me, and she will be converted, and a period of peace
> will be granted to the world.[160]

And then at the last apparition, on June 13, 1929, at Tui,
Lucia described what she saw and heard, saying:

> Under the left arm of the cross, large letters, as if of
> crystal clear water which ran down upon the altar,
> formed these words: "Grace and Mercy." I under-
> stood that it was the Mystery of the Most Holy Trinity
> which was shown to me, and I received lights about
> this mystery which I am not permitted to reveal. Our
> Lady then said to me:
>   "The moment has come in which God asks the Holy
> Father, in union with all the Bishops of the world, to
> make the consecration of Russia to my Immaculate
> Heart, promising to save it by this means. There are

Lucia de Jesus, *Fatima in Lucia's own words*, vol. 1, 22.ª ed. (Fáti-
     ma: Fundação Francisco e Jacinta Marto, 2018), p. 179.

so many souls whom the Justice of God condemns for sins committed against me, that I have come to ask reparation: sacrifice yourself for this intention and pray."

I gave an account of this to the confessor, who ordered me to write down what Our Lady wanted done. Later, in an intimate communication, Our Lord complained to me, saying:

"They did not wish to heed my request! . . . Like the King of France, they will repent and do it, but it will be late. Russia will have already spread her errors throughout the world, provoking wars, and persecutions of the Church. The Holy Father will have much to suffer."[161]

Meditating on these passages will deepen our understanding of the meaning of consecration to Our Lady. Then we will discuss the Consecration of Russia to the Immaculate Heart of Mary.[162]

Consecration: An Invitation to Love

Theologians can sometimes have doubts about the theme of consecration, and to be fair, some of these doubts are perfectly legitimate. Some of them ask whether it is necessary

---

[161]   Ibid., p. 197-98.

[162]   For the theme of the Consecration to the Immaculate Heart of Mary, I was guided by the theological synthesis made by Stefano De Fiores, published in Mariology dictionaries, in the Fatima Encyclopaedia, and specifically *A Consagração como dedicação na Mensagem de Fátima*, José Carlos Carvalho (coord.), (Fátima: Santuário de Fátima, 2014), p. 129-72.

to consecrate ourselves to the Immaculate Heart of Mary since we are already consecrated to God through our baptism? Wouldn't such a Marian consecration be superfluous? Others speculate as to whether it would be appropriate to consecrate *a group of people.* After all, how can a collective consecration be legitimate or effective when many of those consecrated may not even be aware of the consecration? Wouldn't a consecration of this kind violate each individual's free will?

Let us consider first the personal consecration to the Immaculate Heart of Mary, though we will not go into this subject as deeply and thoroughly as some of the most thoughtful theologians have.[163]

At its most basic level, according to Karl Rahner, consecration is an act of love.[164] He says that it is "the attempt to accomplish everything, of being faithful throughout life."[165]

In this willingness to be "faithful throughout life," we seek a fundamental encounter with Mary, the one who is ever-faithful to God. We seek to imitate her and share in her union with Christ. We make a gift of ourselves to be used by her as her Son sees fit, to bring about their designs of mercy upon us. We become collaborators in the salvific mission according to God's plan.

---

[163]   Authors such as St. Luis Maria Grignon de Monfort, St. Maximiliano Kolbe, and St. John Paul II, among others.

[164]   Karl Rahner, A consagração a Maria nas Congregações marianas, in José Carlos Carvalho (coord.), *A Consagração como dedicação na Mensagem de Fátima* (Fátima: Santuário de Fátima, 2014), p. 112.

[165]   Ibid., p. 113.

Consecration to Mary is in fact "embedded" in our consecration to God.[166] The fundamental Christian consecration takes place in baptism, which transmits divine life but also represents the starting point for consecration to Mary. So, consecration to the Immaculate Heart of Mary should not be presented as an initial or isolated act but always within the context of our already ongoing experience of God.

This was the experience that the little shepherds had on May 13, 1917, after their "yes" to the question "Do you want to offer yourselves to God?" In this apparition, they experienced God through the hands of Mary. The moment they said yes was the moment of their personal consecration to the Immaculate Heart of Mary.

Consecration is, therefore, an invitation, an action of God which touches and transforms human beings at the deepest level of who they are. Naturally, the Holy Spirit gives the impetus for such a commitment since it is the Third Person of the Trinity, the Paraclete, who, from Baptism onward, constantly gives Christians the grace to grow closer to God in virtue and love.

The objective of Marian consecration is to help open us further to the Holy Spirit and to be more receptive to the operation of grace in our souls. Consecration is immeasurably valuable because it helps Christians develop some of the features of Marian spirituality—receiving the Word, wishing only to do the will of God, having a humble heart, and perfectly receiving God's salvific will.

---

[166]   Cf. Stefano De Fiores, Consagração, in José Carlos Carvalho (coord.), *A Consagração como dedicação na Mensagem de Fátima* (Fátima: Santuário de Fátima, 2014), p. 156-58.

As Stefano De Fiores explains, "To consecrate oneself to Mary is to allow ourselves to be helped by her example, by her intercession, to find the true meaning of Christian life as defined by Baptism. 'How could we live our Baptism,' says John Paul II, 'without contemplating Mary, the blessed among women, who so beautifully accepts the gift of God? Christ gave her to us as our Mother. Gave her as the Mother of the Church . . . Every Catholic spontaneously entrusts to her their prayers and consecrates to her, to better consecrate to the Lord.'"[167]

From a biblical perspective, the text that serves as the basis for this surrender to Mary is found in the Gospel of John: "And from that hour the disciple took her into his home" (19:27). The way we receive Mary into our homes, which is most fundamentally in our hearts, should be modeled on the beloved disciple's reception of the Blessed Mother into his home, who was doing far more than just providing a place of rest for Mary. Taking her into his home implied opening up to her and her maternal mission; it implied accepting her into the intimate spiritual relationship Christ had already established with him. When we open our hearts to Mary, we do not displace Christ but invite her to help enhance and enrich our already existing relationship with Jesus.

The Consecration of Russia

Regarding the consecration of nations or groups of people, some theologians have said this is possible through the guardianship or mediation principle. What does this mean?

---

[167]   Ibid., p. 159

An analogy may help. Consider the role that parents play in the lives of their children. Parents constantly make decisions for their children without their consent or understanding, such as taking them to school or making them brush their teeth. Parents do these things because they know better than the child, and they know what is best for the child. This situation remains in place until the child reaches a certain age and can be trusted to make his own decisions, which happens gradually over time with different levels of decision making.

This same principle can apply to the consecration of a parish by a parish priest, and a diocese or country by their bishops. As spiritual fathers, priests and bishops act for the wellbeing of their flock's spiritual health. Such a consecration does not violate the freedom of those who do not wish to be consecrated. Since consecration is, essentially, a request for intercessory prayer, it is no more of an infringement upon someone's freedom than to pray for them.

In regards to the consecration Our Lady of Fatima asked for, Lucia began to urge her confessors and the bishop of Leiria in the time period following June 13, 1929. It had been transmitted to her that the moment had come to consecrate Russia to the Immaculate Heart of Mary.[168] But her letters were studied and evaluated by the relevant authorities and the request was slow to get to the pope.

---

[168] In this dimension of consecration to the Immaculate Heart of Mary, I was inspired by the article of Adélio Torres Neiva, Consagração de Portugal e do mundo ao Imaculado Coração de Maria, in José Carlos Carvalho (coord.), *A Consagração como dedicação na Mensagem de Fátima* (Fátima: Santuário de Fátima, 2014), p. 263-91.

On May 13, 1931, seven months after the Fatima apparitions were approved, the whole Portuguese Episcopate came together at the Cova da Iria to preside at a national pilgrimage. At the end of the celebration, the prelates consecrated Portugal to the Immaculate Heart of Mary. This, however, was not precisely what Our Lady had asked for.

In a letter dated May 18, 1936 to Father Goncalves, Lucia writes:

> I have spoken intimately with Our Lord about the matter [consecration of Russia]; and a short while ago I asked Him why He didn't convert Russia without Your Holiness having to consecrate.
>
> *Jesus' reply to Lucia*:
>
> Because I want My whole Church to recognize this Consecration as a triumph of the Immaculate Heart of Mary, so that they may expand its devotion and place, alongside the devotion to My Divine Heart, the devotion to the Immaculate Heart.
>
> *Lucia's reply*:
>
> But My God, the Holy Father will not believe me, if You yourself don't move him through a special inspiration.
>
> *Jesus*:
>
> The Holy Father! Pray very much for the Holy Father. He will do it, but it will be too late! However, the Immaculate Heart of Mary will save Russia, it's been entrusted to Her.[169]

---

[169]   António Maria Martins, *Cartas da irmã Lúcia* (Porto: Editora Livraria Apostolado da Imprensa, 1979), p. 45-46.

In 1937, the Bishop of Leiria conveyed Lucia's request to the pope, and in June of 1938, after their annual retreat, the Portuguese bishops addressed the pope, requesting that "the entire world be consecrated to the same Most Pure Heart [which had saved Portugal], so that it may finally be freed once and for all from all the dangers threatening from all sides, and the peace of Christ may reign in the Kingdom of Christ, through the mediation of the Mother of God."[170]

In October of 1940, Lucia received an order to write directly to Pope Pius XII, which she did on December 2, 1940. She wrote, "In several intimate transmissions, Our Lord has not ceased to insist on this request, lately promising, if Your Holiness would make the consecration of the world to the Immaculate Heart of Mary, with special mention to Russia, and to state that in union with Your Holiness and at the same time the Bishops of the world do it as well, to shorten the days of affliction that He has determined to punish the nations for their crimes, by means of war, famine and various persecutions to the Holy Church and Your Holiness."[171]

Later in the letter, she continues, "Holy Father! If in this union of my soul with God I am not mistaken, Our Lord promises, in consideration of the Consecration of the Nation that the Portuguese Prelates made to the Immaculate Heart of Mary, a special protection to our nation during this war, and that this protection will be proof of the graces

---

[170]   Adélio Torres Neiva, Consagração de Portugal e do mundo ao Imaculado Coração de Maria, in José Carlos Carvalho (coord.), *A Consagração como dedicação na Mensagem de Fátima* (Fátima: Santuário de Fátima, 2014), p. 276.

[171]   Ibid., p. 277.

He would concede other nations if they had equally been consecrated."[172]

On October 31, 1942, Pius XII spoke to the Portuguese people. This radio message ended with the consecration of the world to the Immaculate Heart of Mary.

In the meantime, Lucia continued to insist that Russia specifically needed to be consecrated to the Immaculate Heart of Mary. Pius XII, fully aware that it was necessary to respond to the requests of the Mother of God, finally consecrated Russia to the Immaculate Heart of Mary with the Apostolic Letter *Sacro Vergente Anno* on July 7, 1952, the Slavic people's feast day of Saints Cyril and Methodius. The formal words of the consecration came at the end of the Apostolic Letter: "And we, that our and your prayers and supplications may better be heard and to give you this single proof of our particular goodwill, just as a few years back we consecrated the whole human kind to the Immaculate Heart of the Virgin Mother of God, now in a very special way dedicate and consecrate all the people of Russia to the same Immaculate Heart."[173]

Did this satisfy Our Lord in Lucia's eyes? Not yet! She made it known that this most recent consecration would have been sufficient but that it needed to be done in union with all the bishops of the world.

Paul VI, at the height of the ecumenical council, at the end of the third session, in his speech on November 21,

---

[172]   Ibid., p. 277.

[173]   *A.A.S.* 44, 1952, p. 511, in Adélio Torres Neiva, Consagração de Portugal e do mundo ao Imaculado Coração de Maria, in José Carlos Carvalho (coord.), *A Consagração como dedicação na Mensagem de Fátima* (Fátima: Santuário de Fátima, 2014), p. 281.

1964, in a visible effort to accomplish all the requests of the Virgin of Fatima, referred to the consecration that Pius XII had made, which also did not satisfy Lucia's request. Paul VI did, however, announce that he would be offering the Golden Rose[174] to the Sanctuary of Fatima, this being the only private revelation mentioned at the Second Vatican Council.

Many know the story from here. After Paul VI died, Pope John Paul I was elected, but he reigned for only thirty-three days before he died. His successor, John Paul II, who had throughout his whole life had a great devotion to Our Lady, took with her in mind the papal motto "Totus tuus" (totally yours). Being well versed in the various Marian feast days, he was well aware that May 13 is the feast of Our Lady of Fatima. Consequently, he believed it was providential that his attempted assassination in St. Peter's Square had taken place on May 13 (1981), the anniversary of the first apparition of Our Lady of Fatima. While still recovering from the assassination attempt, John Paul asked that the documents regarding the secret of Fatima be brought to him. Reading them for the first time, he became convinced that Our Lady of Fatima had saved him.

A year later, on May 13, 1982, he went to Fatima to renew the consecration requested by Lucia. John Paul II asked to speak with her before the consecration. Unfortunately, as it

---

[174]   The Golden Rose is a very high Vatican honor (gift) from the Vatican State given to personalities or shrines in recognition of the good done for the sake of humanity. As the name implies, it consists of a branch with flowers, buttons, and leaves carved in gold. The shrine of Fatima has three, offered by Paul VI, Benedict XVI, and Francis.

turned out, he was not able to talk with her until *after* he had performed the consecration, discovering at that time that some aspects of the consecration had not been done properly. In their twenty-minute conversation, he was able to see her point of view.

Then on December 8, 1983, the Feast of the Immaculate Conception, John Paul II wrote a letter to all the bishops of the world inviting them to renew with him, wherever they might find themselves and in whatever way they found most adequate, the consecration of the world to the Heart of Mary. This was to be done on the following Solemnity of the Annunciation of the Lord (1984), because that day would be the close of the Holy Year of Redemption. The wording to be used was similar to his consecration in 1982, but with slight adjustments to align more with what Lucia had advised.

On March 25, 1984, John Paul II made this consecration in Rome before the image of Our Lady of Fatima, which was sent to Rome specifically for the occasion. It was placed near the papal altar, above the tomb of St. Peter. As John Paul had requested, the consecration was renewed by all the bishops around the world. The presence of such collegiality in this consecration was a new characteristic and most significant. To our knowledge, there had never been a consecration made like this by the pope and with all the bishops together.

Though John Paul did not mention Russia specifically in his consecration, leading some to speculate that this consecration had also failed to achieve Our Lady's requests, Lucia assured everyone that it had been well received by heaven. Of this event, she wrote:

This consecration was made, publicly, in Rome, by the
Holy Father, Pope John Paul II, on 25th March, 1984,
before the image of Our Lady of Fatima which is ven-
erated in the Chapel of the Apparitions in the Cova da
Iria, Fatima, and which the Holy Father—after having
written to all the Bishops in the world asking them to
unite themselves with His Holiness in this act of consecration which he was going to make—had ordered
to be brought to Rome for the purpose in order to
emphasize the fact that the Consecration that he was
going to make before this Statue was the one asked for
by Our Lady of Fatima.[175]

Other sources also testify that she insisted the consecration
had been properly carried out. In a conversation with Father
Luis Kondor, when he asked about the validity of the consecration, Lucia replied, "It was done, but it was already
too late!" By this, she meant that Russia had already spread
many of her errors throughout the world. When he asked
her what would signal God's acceptance of the consecration
and the fulfillment of the promise, she replied, "Look to the
east."[176] By this, she simply meant look to Russia, in the east.
In the years following the consecration, the world saw a turn
of events that would culminate in the collapse of the Berlin
Wall in 1989.

---

[175]   Lucia de Jesus, *The message of Fatima: how I see the Message in the
        course of time and in the light of events* (Fátima: Carmelo de Coim-
        bra; Secretariado dos Pastorinhos, 2006), p. 54.
[176]   Carmelo de Coimbra, *A Pathway Under the Gaze of Mary* (Wash-
        ington, NJ: World Apostolate of Fatima, 2015), p. 190.

The Bullet and the Crown

On the occasion of John Paul II's consecration in 1984, in thanksgiving for the role he believed Our Lady had played in saving him, he offered one of the bullets that had been fired during his attempted assassination to D. Alberto Cosme do Amaral, then the Bishop of Leiria-Fatima. Upon receiving it, the bishop asked the same family of the jewelers who had made the crown of Our Lady at the Fatima shrine to consider where to place the bullet.

This crown was very special because it had been made with the jewels of the Portuguese women and offered to the Blessed Mother as a token of thanksgiving for the protection she had given Portugal during World War II. To everyone's great surprise and delight, the bullet fit perfectly in a sort of a hole in the core of the crown. With this last "jewel," the most precious one of all, the statue was finally complete.

When Pope Benedict XVI, John Paul II's successor, came to Fatima on May 12, 2010, he made a touching reference to this bullet in Our Lady of Fatima's crown. Praying at her shrine before the statue of Our Lady, he said, "It is a profound consolation to know that you are crowned not only with the silver and gold of our joys and hopes, but also with the 'bullet' of our anxieties and sufferings."[177]

What an amazing moment! Our pope told the whole world that Our Lady carries not just our joys and triumphs but also our mistakes, our sufferings, our vulnerabilities, our sense of guilt, our wounds, *everything*. The bullet was a symbol of evil in the world, but in her crown, it now symbolizes

---

[177] Benedict XVI, Visit to the Chapel of Apparitions, *Prayer to Our Lady*, May 12, 2010.

God's power and the intercession of Our Lady to triumph over evil and ensure it does not have the last word.

Our Lady's Triumph

So what does the "triumph" of the Immaculate Heart of Mary mean? It is a wonderful, impressive, hopeful, and evocative phrase, but what exactly does it mean in practice?

To answer this, we must look within ourselves, because this triumph takes place in individual hearts. When we answer what she asks us to do, when we pray a daily Rosary, when we do the First Saturday Devotion, when we live with a compassionate spirituality and through the consecration, we bring about her triumph. When we honor her requests at Fatima, we open our hearts steadily to the workings of the Holy Spirit, who forms Christ in us.

This sort of triumph is not a sensational one. But then, the triumph of Jesus's passion and death did not, at that time, seem to be something that would reverberate around the world and for many centuries to come. Why would we expect the triumph of the Immaculate Heart of Mary to be any different?

By strengthening our personal relationship with God, even though this may seem a subtle thing, we are renewing the face of the earth. By changing our hearts, we change the world; we cooperate with God's plan for the world's salvation and bring about peace. In this way, we help to fulfill the mystical and prophetic dimensions of Our Lady's requests at Fatima.

Cardinal Ratzinger made this point with great clarity: "It seems to me that our biggest mistake is to think that only the great economic and political actions can transform the world, it is a temptation—even among Christians—to think that prayer does not have much value and therefore loses its interiority. Now, here in Fatima we hear of things hidden—conversion, prayer, penance—that seem to have no political significance, but are the crucial things, the renewing power of the world.[178]

These words serve as a summary of all that the Virgin Mary came to say in Fatima when she bound together the mystical with the prophetic. With her help, she asks us to change our hearts so that we can change the world!

---

[178]   Cardinal Joseph Ratzinger, Radio Renascença, program *Cartas na mesa* (Cards on the table), October 12, 1996.

Chapter 11

The Spirituality of Francisco

The Enigma of Holiness

Over the next two chapters, we will examine the spirituality, respectively, of Francisco and Jacinta, though let us first begin by making some comments about the children collectively.

To enter into the heart and intimacy of the lives of Jacinta and Francisco is to enter into a mystery, what their own mother describes as "an enigma."[179]

Their life is an enigma in the sense that they lived and acted in a manner that the superficial eye cannot understand. Only if we examine their lives with delicacy and respect can we come to see the deeper meaning of their words and actions. In doing so, we may well find ourselves in awe at the wonders God performed in the lives of these children, the youngest non-martyr saints in the history of the Church. Their lives, their example and witness, challenges each of us to live out the Fatima message as they did.

---

[179] Lucia de Jesus, *Fatima in Lucia's own words*, vol. 1, 22.ª ed. (Fátima: Fundação Francisco e Jacinta Marto, 2018), p. 62.

A Self Offering

In his homily at a Mass celebrated at the Shrine of Fatima on May 13, 2010, Pope Benedict XVI alluded to Francisco's and Jacinta's presence in the long line of the faithful whom God has asked to offer themselves for the good of others: "In sacred Scripture we often find that God seeks righteous men and women in order to save the city of man and he does the same here, in Fatima, when Our Lady asks: 'Do you want to offer yourselves to God, to endure all the sufferings which he will send you, in an act of reparation for the sins by which he is offended and of supplication for the conversion of sinners?'"[180]

Benedict's implication is clear: God is still seeking righteous men and women whom he can count on to save the "city of men." Pope Benedict identifies Jacinta and Francisco as just such people, even though they themselves would never have considered themselves in such an exalted light. However, all of us can see that God made them, as John Paul II said, two candles that illuminated the world amidst a time of darkness, and he wants to do the same with us.

According to the dialogue the children had with Our Lady, what is asked of us is not that we offer things or moments but that we offer *ourselves*. In the first apparition, the angel asked for prayers, and in the second, he asked for prayers and sacrifices. But when Our Lady comes, she asks for everything: "Are you willing to offer *yourselves*?"

Our Lady's request is the most demanding, but also the most beautiful: to offer God not merely some of our tasks or

---

[180]   Benedict XVI, *Homily*, Shrine of Fatima, May 13, 2010.

some of our time, but all of us, our whole heart, our entire lives. It is as if she wants to teach us that in human relationships (as well as in our relationship with God) the value of what we give lies in the extent to which it is a personal gift of ourselves.

The children made just such an offering. They offered their entire selves in saying yes to her request, an echo of her own yes when she was asked by God to offer herself. And just as her yes brought the Word incarnate into the world, the children's yes to the Blessed Mother's requests made them the *message of Fatima incarnate*.

The Truth Behind the "Sad" Faces

Another prefatory comment before we discuss dear little Francisco. I must clear up something that may not seem so important, but it is.

Many people often ask why the three shepherd children of Fatima look so sad or serious, or even angry, in all the photos we have of them. To understand those pictures, we have to consider the specific circumstances in which they were taken.

Francisco, Jacinta, and Lucia were just simple children from poor families living in a small and unknown village. Until the apparitions, their lives were extremely ordinary. They spent their time with family, went to Mass, played games, and tended to their flocks.

Then suddenly, hundreds of people start to confront them and ask them questions. Some who accosted them were believers but still behaved in an aggressive and insistent manner as they went about trying to get information out of them. Others approached the little shepherds with consider-able hostility, trying to prove that they were lying.

Furthermore, the children were unfamiliar with cameras or any other electronic devices; in fact, Fatima didn't even have electricity at that time. Consequently, taking pictures and having one's picture taken were nowhere near as simple as it is today, with just a simple *click*. For anyone to have his or her photo taken involved a drawn-out process in which the "object" of the photo had to stay absolutely still and remain in the same position for a relatively long time (some reports saying as long as twenty minutes!).

Perhaps now we can imagine how taxing it must have been for the three children to be surrounded by so many adults shoving big cameras in their faces and telling them not to move for nearly half an hour. Who could put on a happy face in such a situation?

It is also important to remember the tremendous pressure the children were under. They were subjected to hundreds of questions and interrogations. Some people asked for prayers, and almost everyone wanted them to tell the story over and over again. After several hours of such treatment, anyone would crumble, much less three simple, unschooled chil-dren unfamiliar with strangers or crowds.

So we see that the atmosphere around the children was chaotic, to say the least. In fact, on one occasion, in hopes of getting a relic, a passerby cut off one of Lucia's braids. Would you smile for a photo after someone did this to you? I should think not!

Finally, we should consider the weight of what the chil-dren had seen and learned in the apparitions. They had been given visions of hell and warned of world wars and famines. In this sense, they had to grow up faster than most children.

I am here to tell you the truth about the disposition of these children. According to the testimonies of people who knew Lucia, Francisco, and Jacinta, as well as several other documents we have concerning their personalities, we discover they were actually full of joy. They were playful, as all children are, and prone to play tricks on one another. It is unfortunate that just from looking at a few photos, people can project a somber and serious disposition on them. All accounts of the little shepherds depict happy children rather than strange and serious mystics who went about scowling at everyone. If we hope to ask them to be our friends and to intercede for us, it is important for us to understand who they were on earth, as well as who they still are in heaven.

Thinking About God

So now we see that in many respects, they were ordinary and playful children, and like ordinary children, they had their frailties and limitations. They were not born saints. They had faults and faced difficulties.

Regarding this, Lucia tells us about Francisco's weaknesses:

> In our games he was quite lively; but few of us liked to play with him as he nearly always lost. I must confess that I myself did not always feel too kindly disposed towards him, as his naturally calm temperament exasperated my own excessive vivacity. Sometimes, I caught him by the arm, made him sit down on the ground or on a stone, and told him to keep still; he

obeyed me as if I had real authority over him. Afterwards, I felt sorry, and went and took him by the
hand, and he would come along with me as good-hu-
mouredly as though nothing had happened. If one of
the other children insisted on taking away something
belonging to him, he said: "Let them have it! What do
I care?" . . . My own opinion is that, if he had lived
to manhood, his greatest defect would have been his
attitude of "never mind!"[181]

From this description, it appears that Francisco's greatest
fault might have been his passivity, almost to the point of
being weak or lazy. There is a charm to young men who
are laid back, but if they possess too much of this quality, it
can lead to sloth and indifference. Luckily, Francisco did not
ultimately go down this road.

Of the three children, we know the least about Francisco.
For this reason, he is the last to be understood, at least according to the depths of his contemplative nature and vocation.

My personal relationship with Francisco started on a summer day many years ago, before I became postulator of his
cause, when I was praying by his tomb and noticed a strange
fact. The transfer of the remains of his body to the Basilica
of Our Lady of the Rosary did not happen on the same day
as Jacinta's but occurred one year later.

Why not at the same time? Why one year later?

After I became postulator of their causes, the question was
still there and I challenged myself to find an answer. During
the process of seeking an answer, I came to know him better

---

[181]   Lucia de Jesus, *Fatima in Lucia's own words*, p. 138-39.

and discovered what a special saint we have in this little boy. I discovered how he can be a great source of inspiration for so many of us in this materialistic and fragmented world.

I will give you the answer I found for as to why his remains were sent a year after Jacinta's, but first let us back up. Let us begin our study of Francisco by looking at a short story Lucia revealed for us:

> When we arrived at our pasturage a few days after Our Lady's first Apparition, he climbed up to the top of a steep rock, and called out to us: "Don't come up here; let me stay here alone."
>
> "All right."
>
> And off I went, chasing butterflies with Jacinta. We no sooner caught them than we made the sacrifice of letting them fly away, and we never gave another thought to Francisco. When lunch time came, we missed him and went to call him: "Francisco, don't you want to come for your lunch?"
>
> "No, you eat."
>
> "And to pray the Rosary?"
>
> "That, yes, later on. Call me again."
>
> When I went to call him again, he said to me: "You come up here and pray with me."
>
> We climbed up to the peak, where the three of us could scarcely find room to kneel down, and I asked him: "But what have you been doing all this time?"
>
> "I am thinking about God, Who is so sad because of so many sins! If only I could give Him joy!"[182]

---

[182]   Ibid., p. 144.

This story illustrates Francisco's love for Jesus and serves as a summary of his sanctity. "Thinking about God." Such a simple statement and yet so profound! God was the center of his entire life. How often he repeated: "But what a pity it is that He is so sad! If only I could console Him!"[183]

And when Lucia asked him what he liked to see the best, he answered, "I loved seeing the Angel, but I loved still more seeing Our Lady. What I loved most of all was to see Our Lord in that light from Our Lady which penetrated our hearts. I love God so much."[184]

This was Francisco's life, a little boy totally centered on God. God became the criteria he used to establish his priorities. You might say his "theology" was sound: he loves the angel, but even more Our Lady, but the most, Our Lord. This proper hierarchy was established in his mind and heart. Francisco's clarity, love, and devotion to truth in making God his total focus and the center of his life sets a high bar for all of us. His example teaches us how to order our lives— if we make God the center of our lives, we will know how to establish our priorities. We will know what to do first, next, and last, and what not to do at all.

In my own life, so full of commitments and responsibilities, it is sometimes hard to know what to do first and how to organize all my tasks. In a modern society with so many things demanding our attention (work, family, children, prayer life, rest, holidays, etc.), it is difficult to organize everything. How should we establish our priorities?

---

[183]   Ibid., p. 147.
[184]   Ibid., p. 143.

Francisco gives us our answer: "Think about God." If we do this, we will be prompted to consider his will, which will help organize our lives and prioritize what we have to do. If God is the center of our lives, he will help us understand what is essential and what is secondary. Much of our human suffering comes from spending our time, energy, and enthusiasm on what is secondary, while we often ignore or postpone what is actually essential. This may seem a trivial way to diagnose the cause of human suffering, but often the diagnosis for what ails us can be quite simple.

What are some examples of putting secondary concerns where primary ones would be? How about the many young adults who suffer because they don't look as perfect as models? How about the many people of all ages who worry about how popular they are? What about those whose self-worth is tied up with acquiring the latest brands or technology? Social media has brought a whole new group of secondary concerns that can not only steal our joy but actually make us quite miserable. How many, especially young people, worry incessantly about their *likes* or *followers* on social media? How many compare their photos with those of others? How many worry that, somehow, they are missing out on something? When we measure our joy in terms of such things, we often begin to notice that even success in these areas does not feed our souls.

Francisco, by pointing out the centrality of God, helps us to distinguish what is essential and what is secondary, or even what should be removed completely. Francisco teaches us how to put the essential in the right place, at the center, and then put everything else around it. Some secondary things are worthy of our concern, to be sure, but the question is, what place do these secondary things have? How much space and with what zeal do we put into what is secondary and into what is essential? If you feel confusion over these kinds of matters, drawing everything back to God will bring clarity.

The Hidden Jesus

As mentioned before, Our Lady told the children to go to school to learn how to read. Of course, she was referring to Lucia, since she had said that very soon she would take Francisco and Jacinta to heaven.

As Francisco became more and more sick towards the end of his life, he preferred to do Eucharistic adoration in the church rather than attend school, saying that he wanted to stay with the "Hidden Jesus."

The expression "Hidden Jesus" was how Francisco referred to the real presence of Jesus in the Eucharist, but this expression actually began as a misunderstanding.

It was a tradition at Fatima to have a yearly Corpus Christi procession. The children would dress as angels and throw flowers as the priest went past with the monstrance containing the Host. One year, Jacinta and Lucia got to dress as angels. Lucia tells us:

> At the rehearsals, [Lucia's sister] explained how we were to strew the flowers before the Child Jesus.
>
> "Will we see Him?" asked Jacinta.
>
> "Yes," replied my sister, "the parish priest will be carrying Him."

Jacinta jumped for joy, and kept on asking how much longer we had to wait for the feast. The longed-for day arrived at last, and Jacinta was beside herself with excitement. The two of us took our places near the altar. Later, in the procession, we walked beside the canopy, each of us with a basket of flowers. Wherever my sister had told us to strew the flowers, I strewed mine before Jesus, but in spite of all the signs I made to Jacinta, I couldn't get her to strew a single one. She kept her eyes fixed on the priest, and that was all. When the ceremony was over, my sister took us outside the church and asked:

"Jacinta, why didn't you strew your flowers before Jesus?"

"Because I didn't see Him." Jacinta then asked me: "But did you see the Child Jesus?"

"Of course not. Don't you know that the Child Jesus in the Host can't be seen? He's hidden! He's the one we receive in Communion!"

"And you, when you go to Communion, do you talk to Him?"

"Yes, I do."

"Then, why don't you see Him?"

"Because He's hidden."[185]

And so this was how the children came to refer to the Eucharist as "the Hidden Jesus."

Francisco spent so many hours in adoration that we might say his spiritual school was the tabernacle. At that time, the

---

[185]   Ibid., p. 41.

church was being renovated and the tabernacle was at the entrance of the Church, on a wall in front of the baptismal font. This was where he would spend whole mornings, sometimes as long as three hours, in the greatest intimacy with his friend Jesus, consoling his God.

This might be the most beautiful way to summarize Francisco's brief life that he spent it between the baptismal font and the tabernacle. He lived between baptism and the Eucharist, loving God, being his beloved son and his confidant.

And how intimate their relationship must have become. Lucia tells us:

> He came out of the house one day and met me with my sister Teresa, who was already married and living in Lomba. Another woman from a nearby hamlet had asked her to come to me about her son who had been accused of some crime which I no longer remember, and if he could not prove his innocence he was to be condemned, either to exile or to a term of some years imprisonment. Teresa asked me insistently, in the name of the poor woman for whom she wished to do such a favor, to plead for this grace with Our Lady. Having received the message, I set out for school, and on the way, I told my cousins all about it.
>
> When we reached Fatima, Francisco said to me: "Listen! While you go to school, I'll stay with the Hidden Jesus, and I'll ask Him for that grace."
>
> When I came out of school, I went to call him and asked: "Did you pray to Our Lord to grant that grace?"

"Yes, I did. Tell your Teresa that he'll be home in a few days' time."

And indeed, a few days later, the poor boy returned home.[186]

How intimate must Francisco have been with Jesus that he was able to be so sure that everything would be all right.

Obedience and Humility

Not surprisingly, Francisco also had a very special relationship with Our Lady, and this returns us to the delay of his remains being moved. But before we get to that point, we need to go back a little further.

On the date that Our Lady first appeared in Fatima, May 13, 1917, at approximately noon, the children were playing in the very place where today the basilica stands. They saw what they thought was lightening. Fearing a storm was imminent, they walked down into the valley to go home. But on the place where today rests the Chapel of the Apparitions, they saw another lighting-like strike, followed by the Blessed Mother hovering over a little tree.

According to the testimony of Francisco's mother,[187] he could not see Our Lady at first; only the girls saw, and they fell to their knees. Francisco could not understand what they were doing. When Lucia realized that he could not see Our Lady, she asked why. Our Lady did not answer but rather

---

[186]   Ibid., p. 161.

[187]   Testimony of Olimpia de Jesus, Doc. 80, 09-28-1923, *Selected Fatima documentation – critical edition* (1917-1930) (Fatima: Santuário de Fatima, 2019), p. 297.

told Francisco to pray the Rosary. As soon as Lucia told him to, he immediately started to pray, and at the sixth or seventh Hail Mary, he started to see the Blessed Mother.

This is the moment that inspires me about Francisco and gives me my admiration for him. We can imagine what he was thinking: there's a storm brewing and we have to go home, but the girls are praying in front of a tree, and now I have to pray too? If I had been there, I would have asked for an explanation before even considering to comply: Why me? Why the Rosary? Why now? But Francisco was not like that. He obeyed with simplicity, and that simple obedience allowed him to see.

Lucia gives us another example of his obedience not long after this. After she asks if they will go to heaven, Our Lady says yes for all three of them, but says Francisco must say many Rosaries.[188]

> Afterwards, we told Francisco all that Our Lady had said. He was overjoyed and expressed the happiness he felt when he heard of the promise that he would go to Heaven. Crossing his hands on his breast, he exclaimed, "Oh, my dear Our Lady! I'll say as many rosaries as you want!" And from then on, he made a habit of moving away from us, as though going for a walk. When we called him and asked him what he was doing, he raised his hand and showed me his rosary. If we told him to come and play, and say the rosary with us afterwards, he replied: "I'll pray then as well. Don't

---

[188]   Cf. Lucia de Jesus, *Fatima in Lucia's own words*, p. 175.

you remember that Our Lady said I must pray many
rosaries?"[189]

He was a humble little boy. It seems he was less favored for
whatever reason. He could not see Our Lady at first, he was
the one who never heard her, and we have learned he had
to pray more to get to heaven. But unlike most children, to
whom self-pity comes easily, he never felt sorry for himself.
He never complained. He never compared himself to his
cousin or his sister. He never felt inferior. He accepted who
he was and his mission in this mystery of Fatima.

Isn't this something we need to learn? Our world is one
of fierce competition, filled with jealousy and envy. We are
always competing. We always want to be the best, the tall-
est, the cleverest, with the most money or power or beauty.
This competitiveness instills such anxiety, such competition,
such unhappiness in our lives and in our society. This competitiveness takes place in marriages and families, between
friends, in schools, at work, and even, I am afraid, in spiritual life and in the Church. Francisco teaches us to accept
who we are before God and our role in the history of salvation and simply to do what Our Lady and Jesus ask us.

In one of the books she wrote about Fatima, Lucia reveals
more evidence of Francisco's deep humility. I find the following story particularly touching:

> One day, on our way to the Cova da Iria, when a group
> of people who in order to better see and hear us, set
> Jacinta and myself on top of a wall. Francisco refused
> to let himself be put there, as though he were afraid

---

[189]   Ibid., p. 143.

of falling. Then he leaned against a wall on the opposite side. A poor woman and her son, seeing that they
could not manage to speak to us, went and knelt down
in front of him for a grace. Francisco knelt down also
and asked if they would like to pray the Rosary with
him. They said they would, and began to pray. Very
soon, all those people stopped asking curious questions, and also went down on their knees to pray.[190]

Francisco afraid of falling? Hardly so! Francisco, who loved
to hop around the hills after the sheep, over the rocks of the
mountain, playing his flute on top of so many walls, countless times staying alone on a rock to contemplate the nature
of God and pray his rosary? This boy had no fear of falling.

On the contrary, Francisco wanted no deference which
was not due to him. He accepted his state with simplicity
and never worried about what he was not able to have. He
had a peaceful, gentle, accepting nature.

In this scene, he chooses not to be above others and not
to have them kneel before him. Instead, he chooses to kneel
before God and to pray with those who came to petition
him. The position he chooses is humble, not at the top. And
yet, from his lowly position, he draws others to him. They
are attracted to his humility. When they come, he invites
others to pray the Rosary with him, leading them closer to
Our Lady and to God.

---

[190]   Ibid., p. 162-63.

A Boy and His Rosary

Many have asked me what kind of problems or difficulties .Francisco might have had if he needed to pray more to go to heaven. My personal opinion is that Francisco was no less of a saint than the others. I believe that Our Lady asked Francisco to pray more because he had a contemplative vocation to develop. He was, after all, clearly the most contemplative of the three children.

If, however, Our Lady had told him he had a contemplative vocation to develop, he wouldn't have understood. Instead, she tells him he has to pray many Rosaries to get to heaven. This he understands.

And how does he respond? With obedience, he starts moving away to pray. He prays so much that he develops his contemplative vocation. And he fulfils his mission through the prayer of the Rosary.

The question arises: did he pray enough?

Well, of course he did. The Church demonstrated this with his canonization. But even before that, there is evidence of his strong prayer life.

When it came time in 1951 to move the remains of Jacinta and Francisco to the basilica, there was no doubt as to where Jacinta was to be buried. She had first been laid in the cemetery of Ourem before being transferred to the cemetery of Fatima in 1935. Everyone knew exactly where her plot was in the cemetery.

As for Francisco, he was buried a day after his death on April 5, 1919 in the cemetery of Fatima. His family was very poor and his parents could do little to honor him other than putting a cross over his grave. They did not know that the story was going to unfold the way it did, so they had no reason to think their son would one day become a saint.

When in 1951 Francisco's father, Manuel Marto, was asked to identify his son's burial site, Mr. Marto showed them what he thought was the site. Upon inspection, it turned out this particular plot contained a small casket with the bones of a two- or three-year-old. Clearly, not Francisco. This led to much concern in Fatima.

So, at that point, Jacinta's body was transferred, while the authorities considered what to do about Francisco. His father was insistent about the location, assuring them of the exact plot where his son had been laid.

As it turned out, Francisco's father was actually right. When the young shepherd died in 1919, it was the time of the Spanish flu epidemic, when many children died. Mr. Marto had forgotten that after Francisco's death, another young child had been buried on top of him. When Francisco's father remembered this, the gravediggers dug deeper and found a bigger casket. Inside, they found the remains of Francisco!

How could anyone be sure that the body was his? Because inside, perfectly intact, was his rosary, the rosary with which he prayed throughout his life. There it was. Francisco was identified because of his rosary.

Eventually, scientific tests were also done to prove that the bones in the grave were of a ten- or eleven-year-old boy, but it was the rosary that first identified him. Given Francisco's love of the Rosary and devotion to Our Lady, this is surely no coincidence. God willed that this little boy, who loved the Blessed Mother so much, be identified by his rosary.

A Boy and His Mother

Let us conclude our study of Francisco's spirituality with a closer look at the role the Blessed Mother played in his life. One little story helps us understand his deep relationship with the Mother of God.

On August 13, 1917, when the children were supposed to go visit with Our Lady, the administrator of Ourem took them to jail to interrogate them. He wanted to know the secret. Jacinta began to cry because she was scared and wanted to be with her mother.

But Francisco's only concern was missing their appointment with Our Lady. "Even if we never see our mother again," he said, "let's be patient! We can offer it for the conversion of sinners. The worst thing would be if Our Lady never came back again! That is what hurts me most. But I offer this as well for sinners."[191]

What an extraordinary example of love towards the Blessed Mother! And this explains why, when Our Lady appeared a few days later, on August 19, Francisco was overjoyed.

Despite his youth, Francisco can teach us so much. He teaches us to "think about God," to remain lowly and humble, to be obedient, and to love the "Hidden Jesus" and Our Lady. These are such simple things that can lead to our ultimate happiness if we would just believe in their importance.

---

[191]   Ibid., p. 149.

CHAPTER 12

The Spirituality of Jacinta

To Do the Same as Our Lord

It is now time to get to know Francisco's beloved and adorable sister, who had a spirituality different from his but equally impressive and attractive.

In discussing Jacinta, it might be helpful to revisit a story mentioned earlier in which Lucia says:

> One day on [Jacinta's] way back, she walked along in the middle of the flock. "Jacinta, what are you doing there," I asked her, "in the middle of the sheep?"
>
> "I want to do the same as Our Lord in that holy picture they gave me. He's just like this, right in the middle of them all, and He's holding one of them in His arms."[192]

This is the secret of Jacinta's holiness: she wants "to do the same as Our Lord."

---

[192]   Lucia de Jesus, *Fatima in Lucia's own words*, vol. 1, 22.ª ed. (Fátima: Fundação Francisco e Jacinta Marto, 2018), p. 44.

A Process of Conversion

As was the case with Francisco, Jacinta was not always a perfect little girl. She, too, had her faults.

Lucia even says, "I sometimes found Jacinta's company quite disagreeable, on account of her oversensitive temperament. The slightest quarrel which arose among the children when at play was enough to send her pouting into a corner – 'tethering the donkey' as we used to say. Even the coaxing and caressing that children know so well how to give on such occasions, were still not enough to bring her back to play; she herself had to be allowed to choose the game, and her partner as well."[193]

In the testimony she gave about Jacinta for the canonization process, Lucia describes Jacinta's temperament, explaining, "She was very kind, but she had a fickle temperament, she sulked when she didn't get her way, she had difficulty letting go of what was hers, and she wanted what other children had."[194]

As adults, these descriptions make us smile. Do we not know so many little children just like this? Were *we* not like this ourselves? Are we not perhaps still like this?

It seems the center of Jacinta's life was Jacinta, yet after the apparitions, her very flaws gave rise to her greatest virtues. She allowed herself to be touched by God and human suffering, and in response to the promptings received, she began to change her life, her choices, her attitudes, and her priorities. She opened herself up and allowed herself to be *moved*. The center of her life ceased being herself and became Jesus

---

[193]   Ibid., p. 36-37.

[194]   *Hyacinthae Marto, Positio super virtutibus*, Roma, 1988.

and Mary. The more Jacinta changed, the more she converted, the more we find her at her best, with a generous heart that grows bigger and bigger, sharing all she has with others. She no longer lived for herself but to console Jesus and Our Lady, for the conversion of sinners, for peace in the world, and for the Church and the Holy Father.

Significantly, her greatest flaw—egocentrism—in the hands of the Spirit, turned into her greatest virtue: compassion and solidarity in the good.

My brothers and sisters, this can happen to us too. Just because we have flaws, we should not worry or lose heart! The Spirit can turn those very weaknesses into our greatest virtues. Fidelity to the will of God does not destroy the best in us but brings it out and gives it a richness that, on our own, we would never achieve.

Jacinta had to go through a process of conversion, just as we all do. Of course, her situation—and Francisco's and Lucia's—was somewhat unusual because of the events of Fatima, where an invitation to live a life as a gift for others came from the Mother of God herself. Still, it's worth noting that each of the children had to personally accept this invitation.

In making proper use of Jacinta's freedom, God was able to help her complete the first step of her conversion: not putting herself at the center of her life. This is a slow process for all of us, but it is the key to sanctity. A saint is someone who does not want to be the protagonist of his or her own life but wants God to play the central role.

And so, after the apparitions, through the work of the Holy Spirit, Jacinta's self-centered personality gave way to a little girl with a heart whose main characteristic is compassion, just like Our Lord. Exactly because she wants to "do like him," Jacinta lives a surrendered life, as a gift for others, so that all may have life.

Perhaps one account shows best how she made God and Our Lady rather than herself the center of her life.

When the authorities imprisoned the children in August, Jacinta cried because she missed her mother. This would certainly be normal for any little girl. In the midst of Jacinta's tears, Lucia encouraged her to choose one intention for which to offer up their suffering: either for the poor sinners, for the Holy Father, for peace in the world, or for reparation to the Immaculate Heart of Mary. Despite Jacinta's distress, she did not hesitate to answer: "I'm making the offering for all the intentions, because I love them all."[195]

From then onwards, Jacinta never thought of herself again! God uses suffering in a mysterious way by purifying our self-centeredness. "But surely we know that in everything God works for good for those who love him, who are called according to his purpose" (Rm 8:28).

Jacinta's life was like Jesus's in that she offered herself. She offered herself along with the Immaculate Heart of Mary, for whom she nurtured a very special love. The Immaculate Heart of Mary was little Jacinta's altar, the place of sacrifice where her life was given on behalf of others. She was a shepherdess, like the Good Shepherd, who gives her life for God's sheep.

---

[195]   Lucia de Jesus, *Fatima in Lucia's own words*, p. 53.

Love for Poor Sinners

Of the three shepherd children, Jacinta was the one struck the hardest by the vision of hell during the apparition of July. Lucia tells us:

> Suddenly, she would seize hold of me and say: "I'm going to Heaven, but you are staying here. If Our Lady lets you, tell everybody what hell is like, so that they won't commit any more sins and not go to hell."
>
> To quiet her, I said: "Don't be afraid! You're going to Heaven."
>
> "Yes, I am," she said serenely, "but I want all those people to go there too!"[196]

In order for "everyone to go to heaven," Jacinta was insatiable in her desire to pray and offer sacrifices for sinners. Her soul was burning with this zeal for the salvation of humanity. Everything she did, she offered as an act of love for others, as Our Lady had taught them in July: "Say many times, especially whenever you make some sacrifice: O Jesus, it is for love of You, for the conversion of sinners, and in reparation for the sins committed against the Immaculate Heart of Mary."[197] And Jacinta would add, "And for the Holy Father."[198]

Jacinta knew that to convert sinners and get as many people as she could to heaven, she would have to suffer and

---

[196]   Ibid., p. 126.
[197]   Ibid., p. 178.
[198]   Ibid., p. 50.

make sacrifices. How can we understand this? Why the suffering and the sacrifices?

The "Yes" of Love

To answer this, we need to interpret correctly the sacrificial dimension of the message of Fatima, otherwise we run the risk of turning these three shepherd children into strange children who loved to suffer. Francisco, Jacinta, and Lucia did not love suffering; they loved Our Lord and Our Lady, and through them, loved everything that God loves.

In our day, we need to revisit the whole concept of sacrifice in the light of the Gospel. As is always the case in the Christian life, everything starts with the example given by Jesus. At Fatima, the Holy Spirit, through Mary, invites the children to imitate Jesus, including in his sacrifices and suffering, in order to live it the same way the Lord lived the sacrifice of himself. Under the guidance of the Holy Spirit, Jesus offered himself and his own existence up to the Father. We Christians are called to do as Jesus did, with him, through him.

More than gestures and renunciation, what God wants is our hearts and our lives. What sense would there be in the suffering of those children if there was no love? In fact, suffering for suffering's sake does not make any sense. Jesus did not love the cross, he loved the Father and us, and if, to be faithful to that love, he had to walk until the cross, he accepted it with love. This difference is subtle but essential.

God does not want us to suffer. He did not want it for Jacinta, Francisco, and Lucia either. He wants our love. He wants our hearts. If we are to be like him and to love others the way he did, there will be moments when we are called to sacrifice. These sacrifices can be important as a way to strengthen our will so that we may be prepared to choose good over evil and surrender to God and his will. We are called to surrender to Christ in the cross, not to the cross itself.

Whoever has loved someone understands this sacrificial logic. When we love someone, we must die to self. We sacrifice ourselves when we tell someone, "I love you," not only with words but with gestures that become signs of that love. If we are faithful to love, we will inevitably suffer. How much must a mother and father deny themselves to take care of their infant who does not allow them to sleep? How much suffering can a married couple experience by denying other passions so as to protect their marriage? How many sacrifices must a religious sister make in order to be faithful to her religious vows? The Gospel's perspective on love and suffering is quite clear: fidelity to love carries with it a demand to deny oneself.

In this way, we can understand that the most profound sacrifice is the "Yes" we give to God and to his will. All of our sacrifices flow from this one. The "yes's" we give to our loved ones are just an extension of the larger "Yes" we give to God. Interestingly, this fundamental "Yes" also entails a fundamental "No." "No" to myself. "No" to temptation. "No" to the sin that flows from self-preference. Even sometimes "No" to simple pleasures that are not in themselves sinful.

Often, Jacinta would skip a meal and offer her hunger as a sacrifice for sinners. Her renunciation of a meal perfectly embodies this yes/no phenomenon. "No" to satisfying herself; "Yes" to giving God a sign of her love, both for him and for sinners she had never even met. Jacinta did not refrain from food because she loved hunger but because she loved God and wanted as many people as possible to love him as well. Her sacrifices were expressions of a surrendered life entrusted into the hands of the Father.

The Holy Spirit drives us to love God this way and show it through gestures; it is the love he enlivens in us that prompts us to transform our lives into a living sacrifice. These are the sacrifices pleasing to God. What sense is there for Jacinta to eat bitter acorns or go hungry and thirsty? It only makes sense if it is a gesture of love, a sign to show *the gift of herself* to God.

This is why each of the children, each in their own way, gradually became a living memory of Jesus. The Holy Spirit, through Our Lady and the Angel of Peace, was the one guiding them along this path. From May 13, 1917, from the moment the shepherd children said "Yes," the great sacrifice was the offering of their lives. Like St. Paul said, "I urge you therefore, brothers, by the mercies of God, to offer your bodies as a living sacrifice, holy and pleasing to God, your spiritual worship" (Rom 12:1).

Jacinta lived this confident surrender to God for poor sinners. She was insatiable in finding signs that expressed this surrender. All her life was a gift of self so that others may have life, just as Jesus did. If being consistent with her desire for becoming a gift for the good of others, faithfully living the message of Fatima, brought her difficulties, problems, confusion, then she was willing to accept everything and live as a sign of love and surrender.

We see this self-surrender most clearly in the last months of her life. When the greatest suffering was on the near horizon, Lucia shows us that little Jacinta was ready for her cross:

> On one occasion, [Jacinta] sent for me to come and see her at once. I ran right over.
>
> "Our Lady came to see us," Jacinta said. "She told us she would come to take Francisco to heaven very soon, and she asked me if I still wanted to convert more sinners. I said I did. She told me I would be going to a hospital where I would suffer a great deal; and that I am to suffer for the conversion of sinners, in reparation for the sins committed against the Immaculate Heart of Mary, and for love of Jesus. I asked if you would go with me. She said you wouldn't, and that is what I find hardest. She said my mother would take me, and then I would have to stay there all alone!"
>
> After this, she was thoughtful for a while, and then added: "If only you could be with me! The hardest part is to go without you. Maybe, the hospital is a big dark house, where you can't see, and I'll be there suffering all alone! But never mind! I'll suffer for love of Our Lord, to make reparation to the Immaculate Heart of Mary, for the conversion of sinners and for the Holy Father."[199]

There is a simplicity to this dialogue, but it is in this simplicity that the history of salvation takes place. Jacinta says that Our Lady *asked* her if she still wanted to convert sinners; this

---

[199]   Ibid., p. 59-60.

means God was respecting her free will. Jacinta consented to her suffering with an open heart, just as Christ did. And when Francisco was going to die, Jacinta told him, "Give all my love to Our Lord and Our Lady, and tell them that I'll suffer as much as they want, for the conversion of sinners and in reparation to the Immaculate Heart of Mary."[200]

What a great example from a such a young girl. Whenever someone dear to us is dying, we usually ask him to pray for us in heaven, to take care of us, to walk with us. But Jacinta's request to Francisco was in the other direction. Truly, she was willing to answer the call to love and suffering with a resounding "Yes!"

Last Days

Jacinta eventually fell ill with the Spanish flu and was sent first to a hospital in Ourem, where she was from July 1 to August 31 in 1919. Those who visited her spoke of her joy and peace because she was able to offer sacrifices to God for the conversion of poor sinners.

She was later moved to a hospital in Lisbon, the best pediatric hospital in the country, where they hoped to cure her. But she told everyone who would listen that it was in vain, for she knew she was going to die.[201]

Her diagnosis was serious and life-threatening: pneumonia, a left cavity fistula purulent pleurisy, and osteitis of the

---

[200]   Ibid., p. 60.

[201]   Now that we find ourselves, at the time of this writing, amidst the scourge of the Coronavirus, I cannot help but reach out to Jacinta for her intercession, considering she died almost 100 years prior of a similar sickness and spent her last moments alone. May she comfort all who have suffered from this terrible virus.

seventh and eighth ribs. The treatment was a fissure to drain the pus and a resection of the two ribs under local anesthesia. When the doctor who performed the long and grueling surgery, Dr. Leonardo Costa Freire, was interviewed by the bishop of Leiria, D. Alberto Amaral, he said, "She always gave me the impression of a child with an extraordinary courage." He recalled her "patience, suffering a lot, quiet, silent, never complaining." Considering her age, he thought she showed heroic courage. He was quoted as saying her only words during surgery were, "Oh Jesus! Oh My God!"[202]

For all her life, but especially in these last days with her illness and death, Jacinta's life and death resembled those of Christ. Our Lord did not run from his agony in Gethsemane, or from the loneliness and abandonment on the cross. Likewise, little Jacinta did not reject the loneliness in her illness, nor the deep thirst which consumed her after the operation. She said so many times that she was thirsty, yet it was not possible to give her water. Again, just like Our Lord refusing drink during his passion. She even bore an open wound on her chest in the likeness of the pierced Heart of Jesus, whom she loved so tenderly.

On February 16, 1920, Our Lady appeared to Jacinta and told her she would die.[203] Soon, all her pain disappeared. On the last day of her life, she insisted that the chaplain of the hospital bring her the Hidden Jesus. I presume that because he saw she was looking better, he told her he would bring her Communion the following day. Even after the little girl's insistence, assuring him that she would die that very

---

[202]   *Hyacinthae Marto, Positio super virtutibus*, Roma, 1988.

[203]   February 20 would become the feast days of Jacinta and Francisco.

night, this did not sway the priest. How much dryness and abandonment she must have felt after having been denied Eucharistic Communion, what could have been the only consolation at the hour of her death. As she had predicted, she died that day, alone, at 10:30 p.m.

Despite her suffering and loneliness, Jacinta lived through all these trials with serene joy and in total loving surrender. The similarities between her situation and that of her Savior continued even after her death. Her burial plot was loaned to her family, just as his tomb was. She would only be moved to the Fatima cemetery years later, on September 12, 1935. During the exhumation, her body was photographed and amazingly found to be incorrupt. When Sister Lucia was sent photos of Jacinta in this state, she wrote to the bishop of Leiria to thank him:

> Thank you very much for the photographs. I can never express how much I value them, especially those of Jacinta. I felt like removing the wrappings in order to see all of her . . . I was so enraptured! My joy at seeing the closest friend of my childhood again was so great. I cherish the hope that the Lord, for the glory of the most Blessed Virgin, may grant her the aureole of holiness. She was a child only in years. As to the rest, she already knew how to be virtuous, and to show God and the most holy Virgin her love through sacrifice.[204]

Lucia's joy prompted the bishop to order her to record all she remembered about Jacinta. This, in turn, led to the book *Fatima in Lucia's Own Words*, which we have so often quoted.

---

[204]   Lucia de Jesus, *Fatima in Lucia's own words*, p. 33.

It is fair to say that Jacinta was Fatima's first apostle. Even though, after the first apparition, Lucia told her cousins to say nothing, Jacinta went home and immediately told her mother, and from there, the news spread. Furthermore, Jacinta's incorrupt body set off a chain of events that led to the global spreading of the Fatima story.

A New Kind of Canonization

Some people may think that Francisco and Jacinta were holy or special because they saw the Blessed Mother and that this must have been why they were canonized. We must understand the reason for their holiness and subsequent canonization was not just because they saw the Blessed Virgin Mary. Rather, they were canonized because they were faithful to their baptismal grace and to the mission God entrusted to them.

As Pope Francis observes, "Their holiness is not the consequence of the apparitions, but of their faithfulness and the ardor with which they responded to the privilege of being able to see the Virgin Mary."[205]

Most of us will probably never see Our Lady or Our Lord, but we must nonetheless ask ourselves if we are as faithful to the mission we have been given. The choice is ours. We too can fulfill our missions if we imitate these children and cultivate the same faithfulness and willingness to respond to God's calling.

Before the causes of Francisco and Jacinta for sainthood, there was an understanding in the Church that pre-teenagers

---

205   Pope Francis, *Regina Caeli*, Rome, May 14, 2017.

would not be considered for canonization unless they had been martyrs. The reasoning behind this perspective is that children this young cannot fully, consciously practice virtues in a heroic degree or understand the depths of the faith and everything that comes with it.

Fortunately, this all changed with Francisco and Jacinta. More than three hundred bishops and cardinals from all around the world mailed letters to the Vatican endorsing the shepherd children's canonization. The prelates argued that the children's global fame had already led to many instances of their intercession and that their lives had inspired countless people to seek God.

This led Pope John Paul II in April of 1981 to commission the Congregation for the Cause of the Saints to complete a study on the matter, asking if it was possible for young children to consciously practice virtues in a heroic degree. The congregation concluded that it was possible, and the law was changed, which opened the way to the canonizations of Francisco and Jacinta on May 13, 2017. This was a great celebration for the Church not just because of the canonization of the youngest non-martyred saints in history but also because it proclaimed a deeper understanding about the sanctity of children, which will eventually lead to more canonizations of young saints. Furthermore, through these canonizations, the Church took a concrete action to show that the universal call to holiness is, as *Lumen Gentium* (*Light of the People*) had specified, *truly* universal. This call includes children!

As we have seen, God's grace radiates intensely from these two child saints. This highlights the gift of children and the duty we have to protect their innocence and purity, which are so often threatened in our society. Pope Francis made this point when he explained, "With the canonization of Francisco and Jacinta, I wanted to propose to the entire Church their example of bonding with Christ and their evangelic witness, and I also wanted to urge the entire Church to take care of children."[206] In them, as the Holy Father said, we can "re-discover the young and beautiful face of the Church."[207]

Francisco, the contemplative one, and Jacinta, the compassionate one, are the spiritual summation of what the Church is continually called to be: contemplative and compassionate. And because they were able to make present the prophetic force of love, with their witness and their solidarity with history, the lives of Francisco and Jacinta will never belong to the past.

Blessed with the light that shines through their lives, may each one of us feel moved to a greater love for God, for the Church, and for humanity through the Immaculate Heart of Mary.

---

[206] Ibid.

[207] Francis, *Homily*, Shrine of Fatima, May 13, 2017, Canonization of Francisco and Jacinta.

CHAPTER 13

Lucia: The One Left Behind

A Heart that Beats for God Alone

Very early on, before any of the apparitions began, Lucia had a spiritual experience that showed how Our Lady was going to shape her life. This event occurred during her first confession which prepared her to receive her First Holy Communion:

> When my turn came round, I went and knelt at the feet of our dear Lord, represented there in the person of His minister, imploring forgiveness for my sins. When I had finished, I noticed that everyone was laughing. My mother called me to her and said: "My child, don't you know that confession is a secret matter and that it is made in a low voice? Everybody heard you! There was only one thing nobody heard: that is what you said at the end."
>
> On the way home, my mother made several attempts to discover what she called the secret of my confession. But the only answer she obtained was complete silence. Now, however, I am going to reveal

222

the secret of my first confession. After listening to me, the good priest said these few words: "My child, your soul is the temple of the Holy Spirit. Keep it always pure, so that He will be able to carry on His divine action within it." On hearing these words, I felt myself filled with respect for my interior, and asked the kind confessor what I ought to do.

"Kneel down there before Our Lady and ask her, with great confidence, to take care of your heart, to prepare it to receive Her beloved Son worthily tomorrow, and to keep it for Him alone!"

In the Church, there was more than one statue of Our Lady; but as my sisters took care of the altar of Our Lady of the Rosary I usually went there to pray. That is why I went there on this occasion also, to ask her with all the ardor of my soul, to keep my poor heart for God alone. As I repeated this humble prayer over and over again, with my eyes fixed on the statue, it seemed to me that she smiled and, with a loving look and kindly gesture, assured me that she would. My heart was overflowing with joy, and I could scarcely utter a single word.[208]

Clearly, from Lucia's earliest years, Our Lady was gently working to shape the heart of this young girl, ensuring it would be a heart that beats for God alone.

---

[208]   Lucia de Jesus, *Fatima in Lucia's own words*, vol. 1, 22.ª ed. (Fátima: Fundação Francisco e Jacinta Marto, 2018), p. 71.

Three Defining Moments

We do not have the space here to make a thorough analysis of Lucia's biography and spiritual journey. However, we can briefly describe three moments that shaped the direction her life would take:

1. **May 13, 1917**, when she gave her life to God
2. **June 13, 1917**, when she received her mission to spread the message of Fatima
3. **June 15, 1921**, when she understood the importance of being in full communion with the Church

Though many moments no doubt formed Lucia's sanctity, these three defining occasions occurred very early in her life and had a tremendous impact on her. Let us examine each briefly before going into more detail later.

It all started on that Sunday morning, May 13, 1917, when "the lady brighter than the sun" asked Lucia and her cousins, "Are you willing to offer yourselves to God and bear all the sufferings He wills to send you, as an act of reparation for the sins by which He is offended, and of supplication for the conversion of sinners?"

Lucia answered, "Yes, we are willing." To which Our Lady replied, "Then you are going to have much to suffer, but the grace of God will be your comfort."[209]

From here, we know the story well. Jacinta could not keep quiet and the whole town learned what had happened. This began Lucia's sufferings, chiefly through the doubt of her mother. In this state of affairs, tired and afflicted, Lucia asked

---

[209]   Ibid., p. 175.

Our Lady in June to take her to heaven. We know that after Our Lady promised to take Francisco and Jacinta, Lucia's mission became clear: she would be the one left behind.

Our Lady told her, "You are to stay here some time longer. Jesus wishes to make use of you to make me known and loved. He wants to establish in the world devotion to my Immaculate Heart."[210]

Years later, Lucia would comment on this: "It was the mission God had for me; but having been left without the company of Francisco and Jacinta it seemed to me that I was left alone in this world so uncertain and barren, with no one to follow me, understand me, help me and share with me."[211]

Memorably, Lucia asked Our Lady, "Am I to stay here alone?"

Mary's answer was immediate: "No, my daughter. Are you suffering a great deal? Don't lose heart. I will never forsake you. My Immaculate Heart will be your refuge and the way that will lead you to God."

At that point, Lucia says, "It was then that the heavenly Messenger, opening her arms with a gesture of maternal protection, enfolded us in the reflection of the immense Light of the Being of God."[212]

Though only ten years old, Lucia was forever marked by that "immense Light of the Being of God."

---

[210] Ibid., p. 177.

[211] Lucia de Jesus, *The message of Fatima: how I see the Message in the course of time and in the light of events* (Fátima: Carmelo de Coimbra; Secretariado dos Pastorinhos, 2006), p. 43.

[212] Ibid., p. 44.

Four years later, when Lucia was fourteen, another significant moment occurred. The bishop of Leiria, D. José Alves Correia da Silva, began to worry about her education. He decided that she should leave Fatima, go to Porto, and enroll at the Sisters of Saint Dorothy school. Lucia was saddened at the prospect of leaving everything she knew and everyone she loved behind. Though she at first agreed to go, she then had doubts. She visited the Cova da Iria and determined that she would *not* submit to the bishop's request.

It was then that Lucia says, "I felt your friendly and maternal hand touch me on my shoulder and your voice brought back the peace to my soul: 'Here I am for the 7th time, go follow the way the Bishop wants to take you, that is the will of God.'"[213]

This is the seventh apparition of Our Lady to Lucia, fulfilling the promise she made on May 13, 1917, when she said, "Afterwards, I will return here yet a seventh time,"[214] and indeed she came on this day, June 15, 1921. This seventh visit helped teach Lucia how much heaven values obedience to the Church.

At each of these junctures, Lucia's life and mission consisted of a surrender to God, a consecration to him so she could spread the message of Fatima throughout the world, and a life lived in full communion with the Church. It is upon these three pillars that the rest of her life would be built.

---

[213]   Blessed Francisco and Jacinta Marto, Bulletin of the Shepherd Children, January-March 2006.

[214]   Lucia de Jesus, *Fatima in Lucia's own words*, p. 175.

Becoming a Carmelite

From very early on and after the experiences of the apparitions, Lucia was attracted to the religious life, specifically to Carmelite spirituality. In the last apparition of October, during the miracle of the sun, we get a glimpse of how Divine Providence may have been drawing her to a Carmelite life. Lucia recounts,

> After Our Lady had disappeared into the immense distance of the firmament, we beheld St. Joseph with the Child Jesus and Our Lady robed in white with a blue mantle, beside the sun. St. Joseph and the Child Jesus appeared to bless the world, for they traced the Sign of the Cross with their hands. When, a little later, this apparition disappeared, I saw Our Lord and Our Lady; it seemed to me that it was Our Lady of Sorrows. Our Lord appeared to bless the world in the same manner as St. Joseph had done. This apparition also vanished, and I saw Our Lady once more, this time resembling Our Lady of Mount Carmel.[215]

This vision of Our Lady of Mount Carmel remained in Lucia's heart, spurring her towards her vocation as a Carmelite nun.

However, the first years of her religious life were spent as a Dorothean, at the institute that had welcomed her as a student in 1921. She would remain a Dorothean for twenty-three years. However, constant visits because of her fame proved to be a distraction. They made it difficult to find

---

[215]   Ibid., p. 183.

silence and time for prayer. In accord with her desire for the opportunity to spend more time in contemplation, she urged the bishop to move her.

Finally, on March 25, 1948, she was allowed to enter the Carmel of Saint Teresa in Coimbra, receiving her habit on May 13 of that same year. It was here that Lucia found her home, the ideal atmosphere where she developed her initial vocation given to her by God through the hands of Our Lady. In the silent intimacy of the convent and entrusted into the hands of God, she would become a prophet of the Mother of the Most High, a prophet for our age so distraught and thirsting for Light and Truth. Lucia's Carmelite vocation was how she fulfilled the mission given to her in Fatima, where she offered herself to God for humanity, and became a messenger announcing the triumph of the Immaculate Heart.

The masters of Carmel pointed the way. Emulating John of the Cross, she saw love as her only mission. His words would certainly have resonated with the young Carmelite when she prayed the Spiritual Canticle (28):

> Now I occupy my soul
> and all my energy in his service;
> I no longer tend the herd,
> nor have I any other work
> now that my every act is love.

Lucia left her Carmelite convent only on seldom occasions. She did go to Fatima each time a pope visited and left occasionally to help oversee the construction of other Carmelite convents in Portugal. She also went out for medical appointments and to vote in political elections.

It was these last occasions when people would flock to see her. Each time there was an election, Lucia knew that many people, often with their young children, would come to take pictures with her, or ask her to touch their children. Television and news studios would also seek her out and photograph or film her without her permission.

This was a burden for her, but after a meeting with John Paul II in May of 1991, she learned from him: "When we have no option but to let them do it, we give them that pleasure."[216] He helped her see that, in most cases, people flocked to them as a means of drawing closer to God, and so it was a duty they must, on occasion, learn to deal with.

But most of Lucia's time was spent in the quiet of the convent. Her Carmelite life was her way to God, her path to holiness. And though she rarely went out into the world, she still found a way to fulfill her mission of spreading devotion to the Immaculate Heart of Mary.

Spreading the Message

Sister Lucia's main concern, her great mission, was always to spread the message of Our Lady. To do this, she was not afraid to approach religious and civil authorities whenever she deemed it necessary to ensure that the requests of Our Lady would be heard and fulfilled.

The carrying out of this mission unfolded throughout her long life, which encompassed some of the most dramatic and decisive moments of the twentieth century, in the world and in the Church. She witnessed the Spanish Civil War

---

[216]   Lucia de Jesus, *O Meu caminho*, October 6, 1991.

(1936–1939), World War II (1939–1945), the Second Vatican Council (1962–1965), and the Cold War (1947–1991).

Lucia read all these events through the prism of Fatima. How much more did these events mean to her, who had seen a vision of hell and "a city in ruins," than to the average person? Yet, she also would have viewed these events from the perspective of devotion to the Immaculate Heart of Mary, and a firm belief in the triumph of Our Lady's Heart. Lucia's message was a ray of hope and mercy for a world afflicted with every kind of suffering and confusion.

Lucia spread this message through the ministers of the Church which Providence placed in her path, as well as through her own writings. At the behest of her bishops, she penned several books, including *Fatima in Lucia's Own Words I*, *Fatima in Lucia's Own Words II*, *Calls from the Message of Fatima*, *How I See the Message in the Course of Time and in the Light of Events*. Of all these books, the first was the best seller, with over several million sold worldwide and translated into nineteen languages. Few authors in the Church and the world have been so widely read, commented on, and criticized as Lucia de Jesus.

But her activity as a writer was not confined only to these publications. There is also her diary, *O Meu Caminho (My Way)*, which, possibly more than all the other writings we have of hers, serves as a witness to her intimate life with God, as well as to the many recorded moments of her life.

Still more, there are the immense number of letters she wrote. From 1970 onwards, more than seventy thousand letters came to her in her Carmelite convent, arriving from all parts of the world. She took the time to respond to many of

them, despite her busy schedule. What is particularly interesting is the identity of her correspondents. In some cases,
it was the pope himself, including John XXIII, Paul VI, and
John Paul II. Other times, it was future saints, like Josemaria
Escriva and Teresa of Calcutta. Perhaps most often, however,
those who wrote to Lucia were everyday, unknown people in
need of hope and assurance of God's love for them. She even
exchanged letters with people of other faiths, including a
Protestant pastor and a Buddhist! Unfortunately, she burned
some of these letters out of "prudence and respect for the
reputation of the people who wrote them,"[217] but thankfully,
many of the letters survive to this day.

As in all her other efforts, Lucia's letters sought to spread
the message of Fatima and propagate the requests of Our
Lady, especially for prayer and conversion. For Lucia, these
letters were "a witness to the faith and the power of prayer
and of God's grace working in the souls and His action
through the Message of Our Lady to the world."[218] Lucia
knew that people came to her not because of her own merits
but because of Our Lady. Lucia sought to give each of those
with whom she corresponded a sisterly word, ensuring them
that the Virgin Mother loves them and takes them into her
heart.

Lucia's face-to-face visits were limited by the Holy See to
some extent. There were several reasons for this. The popes'
first concern was to protect her and enable her to live out
her life as a Carmelite. It is clear, though, that they also
wanted to protect her from people who spoke about Fatima

---

[217]   Lucia de Jesus, *O Meu caminho*, October 18, 1983.
[218]   Lucia de Jesus, *O Meu caminho*, April 15, 1981.

maliciously, spreading erroneous interpretations and even lies about the seer herself.

Nonetheless, many did come to see her, including almost fifty cardinals and countless bishops from all over the world, in addition to kings, heads of state, ambassadors, film stars and directors, as well as the humble and simple workers who performed services in the convent. Regardless of their status, they all shared with her their pain, suffering, and anxieties, the drama of their lives and responsibilities.

Recognizing this aspect of Sister Lucia's vocation, the magazine *Flama* wrote about her in 1967: "Whoever keeps a secret in the proportion of the Message of Fatima, keeps in her heart the whole world. Lucia, in the very strict cloister of the Carmel of Coimbra, has within her hundreds and thousands of souls who speak all languages, who belong to all continents and oceans. She is never alone, as insurmountable as the walls of the Monastery of Saint Teresa might be."[219]

Indeed, we can apply to Lucia what the Church said of its own mission in that wonderful Vatican Council II document *Gaudium et spes* (*The Joy and Hope*): "The joys and the hopes, the griefs and the anxieties of the men of this age, especially those who are poor or in any way afflicted, these are the joys and hopes, the griefs and anxieties of the followers of Christ. Indeed, nothing genuinely human fails to raise an echo in their hearts."[220]

Just as the Church bears the pains of the last two centuries, so Lucia did as well on a personal level despite being

---

[219] Magazine *Flama*, September 15, 1967.
[220] Second Vatican Council, *Gaudium et spes* (1973), no. 1.

hidden away in her convent. She, like the Blessed Mother, carried the pain of the world in her heart.

A Humble Instrument

Lucia once wrote, "My soul is an ocean of memories, responsibilities, which I feel before a Message that God wanted to entrust to me and of which I do not feel worthy, incapable of projecting it the way God wanted it to be done."[221]

The humility evident in this comment was one of her main characteristics—and it was this virtue that enabled her to fulfill her mission. Whatever attention she received, she immediately directed to Our Lady and Our Lord. All was done for them and by them. As she always recognized, she was simply their instrument:

> Very well then. I need no more than this: obedience and abandonment to God who works within me. I am truly no more than a poor and miserable instrument which He desires to use, and in a little while, like a painter who casts his now useless brush into the fire so that it may be reduced to ashes, the Divine Artist will Himself reduce His now useless instrument to the ashes of the tomb, until the great day of the eternal Alleluias. And I ardently desire that day, for the tomb does not annihilate everything, and the happiness of eternal and infinite love begins – now![222]

She knew God made use of instruments like her to "show us that the work is His, and that it is He . . . who implements

---

[221]   Lucia de Jesus, *O Meu caminho*, May 13, 1968.
[222]   Lucia de Jesus, *Fatima in Lucia's own words*, p. 137.

the plans of His infinite mercy."[223] And she vowed to "remain in the museum of the world, reminding all who pass, not of misery and nothingness, but of the greatness of the Divine Mercies."[224]

It was also Lucia's humility that allowed her to submit to the authority of the Church on so many of the complicated matters in the midst of which she found herself. Her filial respect for the Church can be summarized by these words from her book *The Message of Fatima*: "I do not know if what I say here is quite what it should be. If Holy Church says something else, believe in the Church and not what I say, for I am poor and ignorant, and I may be wrong. This is what I think and not what I know, for I know nothing except to love and serve God and our neighbor for God's sake."[225]

To some, it may seem surprising that a humble shepherd child, who became a simple religious sister in a cloister, was entrusted with spreading this far-reaching salvific message. But it is in humility like Lucia's that the light of God shines best. She "hid" within her cloister so that the light of the message could shine brightly. Like John the Baptist, Lucia's life teaches us that "he must increase but I must decrease" (Jn 3:30).

Considering how frequently the modern world misunderstands the nature of humility, perhaps it would be helpful to emphasize that humility and meekness should not be confused with weakness. Lucia was a woman with a sharp awareness of her mission, a mission to which she would be

---

223   Lucia de Jesus, *The message of Fatima*, p. 57.
224   Lucia de Jesus, *Fatima in Lucia's own words*, p. 192.
225   Lucia de Jesus, *The message of Fatima*, p. 35.

faithful until her last days. She was bold and courageous and nothing held her back when it came to announcing what Our Lady had told her.

Like all the saints, she remained humble while acting with fortitude and perseverance in building up the Kingdom of God. Her interactions with several different popes exemplify the way she maintained this balance. In the presence of the Holy Father, Lucia knew her place and always acted with obedience, but she was also unafraid to honestly advise on how the consecration was to be carried out according to Our Lady's wishes. In fact, if she had not been so persistent in getting it right, the consecration of John Paul II, which heaven accepted, would never have come to pass.

Nothing held Lucia back from announcing what she had heard from Our Lady. Even if we only hear Lucia through her books and letters, her voice will reach the ends of the earth. May we emulate her "humble strength" every day as we fulfill our own callings.

Obedience to Holy Mother Church

Throughout this book, we have mainly concentrated on the primary apparitions of Fatima, those being of the Angel of Peace in 1916 and of Our Lady in 1917, 1925, and 1929. But now, let us contemplate a bit more the seventh apparition, which occurred to Lucia only and helped form her obedience to Holy Mother Church.

When Bishop José Alves Correia da Silva met Lucia for the first time around 1920 and 1921, he questioned her about the events she had witnessed. As mentioned earlier, he suggested she leave Fatima for Porto so that she could attend school. He also suggested the move because he wanted to protect her from the thousands of pilgrims coming to Fatima every year who were eager to see Lucia or talk with her.

At first, Lucia was agreeable to this plan, but soon she began thinking of all she would leave behind: "The joy I had felt when I left the Bishop didn't last long. I started thinking of my family, my parents' house, Cova da Iria, Cabeço, Valinhos, the well, and leave everything? Forever? To go I don't know where? I said yes to the Bishop, but now I will say that I changed my mind and I don't want to go there."

In the midst of this turmoil, she went to the Cova da Iria, where Lucia records that the Blessed Mother miraculously appeared once again:

> So helpful, once again you have come down to earth; and then I felt your helping hand and maternal touch on my shoulder. I looked up and I saw you, it was you, Blessed Mother holding my hand and showing me the path, and your lips unveiled the sweet timbre of your voice and light and peace was restored to my soul. "Here I am for the seventh time. Go, follow the path which the Bishop wants to take you, that is the will of God." I repeated then my "yes" now much more conscious than on that day on May 13, 1917. And while you went up to heaven once again, in a glance, the marvels that in that very place just four years ago I had been able to contemplate, went through my soul.[226]

---

[226]   Blessed Francisco and Jacinta Marto, Bulletin of the Shepherd Children, January-March 2006.

Before Lucia moved to Porto, she was exhausted and full of distress. She was dealing with family issues and the pilgrims constantly flocking to her, and there was tremendous pressure on her because of all that had happened. Additionally, Francisco and Jacinta had died, leaving her all alone to deal with it all. Yet at the same time, she was longing for the past and sorry to leave her beloved home and family. It caused her great suffering to think of leaving Fatima, and she feared the future and the unknown. She wanted to say, "No! I am staying put!"

Most of us can probably relate to this sentiment. Often when a new calling or endeavor comes up, we hesitate to accept it. We long for the past and what we are comfortable with, and we fear the unknown of the future. Following a call that comes from God is not always peaceful or without difficulty. There is a temptation to refuse God's plan for us.

We can learn from Lucia at these moments. Unlike her, we may not receive assurance from the Mother of God in the form of an apparition, but we can do what Lucia did when she was confused: pray! She went back to the place where it all began. She went to the Cova da Iria to pray and seek Our Lady's guidance and the Lord's will.

Lucia's example reminds us that during difficult moments, we must always have recourse to prayer. It is one of the best ways to obtain understanding in the midst of confusion. It is also important to note that praying by no means ensures we will get what we want or get an answer that we find easy to follow. Our Lady did not give Lucia the answer she wanted; she did not tell Lucia that she could do as she pleased and stay in Fatima. Our Lady did not make life easier.

Nonetheless, Lucia was full of peace about the situation. Such peace is often the fruit of our prayer, not a removal of what pains us but a strength and clarity as to how to persevere. Prayer helps us to better understand the way of God rather than changing his ways. In her prayer about whether or not to go to Porto, Lucia received just such strength and clarity, through Our Lady's prompting to obey the dictates of her Son's Church. This is the beauty of Fatima, that we learn, through our mother, how to obey our Father.

So Lucia renewed the "Yes" she gave to Our Lady years earlier with a another "Yes" to the Church, going to Porto as the bishop had requested. This became a pattern. A first "Yes" to her calling, and many repeated "Yes's" in the many small acts of which her long life was woven. She would obey, even in the midst of so many challenges, her prioress, the provincial of the Carmelite Order in Portugal, the bishop of Coimbra, the bishop of Leiria-Fatima, the nuncio in Portugal, and the Vatican. We can truly say that she become a living example of the obedience of Jesus, who "learned obedience from what he suffered" (Heb 5:9).

In speaking of Lucia's obedience to the Church, we should mention her special relationship with and love for the Holy Father. As mentioned earlier, she had a relationship with many popes, but for Lucia, any pope was always the Vicar of Christ and she treated them all with the same respect and reverence.

Obviously, what she saw in the third part of the secret, with the bishop in white being persecuted, engendered a great love for him and led her to offering many prayers and sacrifices on his behalf. Her correspondence with each pope usually began through an act of obedience by answering certain questions pertaining to Fatima, but it often became a friendship and a special spiritual union, especially with John Paul II. History and Providence united them on May 13, 1981, the day of his assassination attempt. This first brought them together and they never failed to stay in touch. It is moving to see the spiritual friendship of these two giant figures of the twentieth century. They wrote letters to one another, sent gifts, asked each other for prayers, and met in person on a few special occasions.

A Bridge Between Fatima and Heaven

As Providence would have it, the end of their lives were woven together as well. Both fell ill and died two months apart in 2005. As each lay dying, they prayed for each other. Lucia clung tight to a rosary John Paul had given her as a birthday gift the year before, and she eventually died with it in her hands. One of her last acts was to read a message John Paul had sent her, a friendly word from one who recognized that their paths had crossed in the Immaculate Heart of Mary: "Reverend Sister Lucia of Jesus and the Immaculate Heart, I was informed of the state of your health. I come to affirm our affectionate union with a special remembrance of your personal union with God, with all the comfort to help you overcome these worthily resigned serene moments of trial united to Christ the Redeemer, and let yourself be enlightened by his Easter. As a pledge of the best heavenly

graces, I send to you and the Carmelite Community and families my apostolic blessing."[227]
Also impressive is the message his Holiness sent to the bishop of Coimbra the day after Lucia's death, February 14, 2005:

> Venerable Brother Albino, Bishop of Coimbra, with deep emotion I learned that Sister Maria Lucia of Jesus and Immaculate Heart, 97 years old, was called by the heavenly Father to the eternal mansions of heaven. She reached the goal for which she always aspired in prayer and silence, in the convent. . . . The visit of the Virgin Mary that little Lucia received in Fatima, along with her cousins Francisco and Jacinta in 1917, was for her the beginning of a unique mission to which she remained faithful until the end of her days. Sister Lucia leaves us with an example of great fidelity to the Lord and of joyful adherence to His divine will. I remember with emotion the various meetings I had with her and the bond of spiritual friendship that over the time became more intense. I have always felt supported by the daily gift of her prayers, especially in the hard times of trial and suffering. May the Lord reward her amply for her great and hidden service to the Church.[228]

---

[227]   Carmel of Coimbra, *A Pathway Under the Gaze of Mercy* (Washington, NJ: World Apostolate of Fatima), 2015, p. 421.
[228]   Ibid., p. 426–27.

With his gratitude for her "hidden service to the Church," John Paul intuited that her greatest spiritual desire was to be "a hidden stone in the foundation of the Holy Church."[229]

The Portuguese government understood the importance of Lucia de Jesus for their country and declared February 15 a national day of mourning. Her funeral was a significant event, with national TV coverage. The Portuguese episcopal conference was present, and the patriarch of Lisbon, D. José Policarpo, shared a memorable message: "We are moved, not so much because she died, but because today between Fatima and heaven a new bridge has been established."[230]

Lucia's greatest wish was to be faithful to the "yes" she gave Our Lady in 1917 and to the mission God had entrusted her with when she was a little girl. She spent nearly a century bringing the light of Jesus, the light Our Lady radiated to her and her cousins all those years ago, to all of us. She sought "to live in the light, to live for the light, to live from the light."[231]

And this she did well. With her long race now ended, she serves as a powerful intercessor and a source of inspiration for all who love the Immaculate Heart of Mary.

---

[229] Lucia de Jesus, *O Meu caminho*, May 8, 1965.
[230] José Policarpo, Homily, Funeral of sister Lucia, February 15, 2005.
[231] Lucia de Jesus, *O Meu caminho*, June 18, 1970.

CONCLUSION

A Mantle of Light

Everything in Fatima speaks to us of light, and this is
something our papal leaders have helped us to see.

Pope St. John Paul II spoke of Saints Francisco and Jacinta
as "two candles which God lit."[232] Pope Benedict XVI stated
"that Light deep within the shepherd children, which comes
from the future of God, is the same Light which was mani-
fested in the fullness of time and came for us all: the Son of
God made man."[233]

Touched by the candlelight procession in the Sanctuary of
Fatima, Benedict addressed the people further, saying:

> All of you, standing together with lighted candles in
> your hands, seem like a sea of light around this sim-
> ple chapel, lovingly built to the honor of the Mother
> of God and our mother, whose path from earth to
> heaven appeared to the shepherd children like a way
> of light. However, neither Mary nor we have a light
> of our own: we receive it from Jesus. His presence
> within us renews the mystery and the call of the burn-
> ing bush which once drew Moses on Mount Sinai and

---

[232] John Paul II, Homily May 13, 2000, Beatification of the Little
Shepherds, Sanctuary of Fatima.

[233] Benedict XVI, Homily May 13, 2010, Sanctuary of Fatima.

still fascinates those aware of the light within us which burns without consuming us (cf. Ex 3:2–5).[234]

And Pope Francis, our current pontiff, speaks of Fatima as a mantle of light: "In Lucia's account, the three chosen children found themselves surrounded by God's light as it radiated from Our Lady. She enveloped them in the mantle of Light that God had given her. According to the belief and experience of many pilgrims, if not of all, Fatima is more than anything this mantle of Light that protects us."[235]

At another instance, Francis added, "Let us be guided by the Light which comes from Fatima. May the Immaculate Heart of Mary always be our refuge, our consolation and the path that leads to Christ."[236]

Light! Light! Light!

For us, heirs to all that has happened in the more than a century since the first events of Fatima, it is up to us to be witnesses to and reflections of this light, which is Christ Jesus, Lord of time and history.

---

[234]   Benedict XVI, Recitation of the Holy Rosary, Chapel of the Apparitions, Sanctuary of Fatima, May 12, 2020.

[235]   Francis, *tweet*, May 13, 2017.

[236]   Francis, *Regina Caeli*, May 14, 2017.

Bibliography

Sources

Carmel of Coimbra – A Pathway under the gaze of Mary. Washington, NJ: World Apostolate of Fatima, 2015.

JESUS, Lúcia de – *Fatima in Lucia's own words. Vol. 1.* 22nd ed. Fátima: Fundação Francisco e Jacinta Marto, 2018.

_____ *Fatima in Lucia's own words. Vol. 2.* 6th ed. Fátima: Fundação Francisco e Jacinta Marto, 2017.

_____ *"Calls" from the message of Fatima.* 8th ed. Fátima: Secretariado dos Pastorinhos, 2017.

_____ *The message of Fatima: how I see the Message in the course of time and in the light of events.* Fátima: Carmel of Coimbra; Secretariado dos Pastorinhos, 2006.

Selected Fatima documentation – critical edition (1917-1930). Fatima: Shrine of Fatima, 2019.

Studies

ANTUNES, Virgílio – Conhecer, viver e difundir a mensagem de Fátima. In COUTINHO, Vítor (coord.). *Mensagem de Esperança para o mundo: Acontecimento e significado de Fátima*. Fatima: Shrine of Fatima, 2012, p. 151-162.

BOFF, Clodovis – Fátima: a mais política das aparições marianas. In COUTINHO, Vítor (coord.). *Mensagem de Esperança para o mundo: Acontecimento e significado de Fátima*. Fatima: Shrine of Fatima, 2012, p. 167-237.

BUENO DE LA FUENTE, Eloy – Dimensão teocêntrica da mensagem de Fátima: o esplendor da Trindade. In COUTINHO, Vítor (coord.). *Mensagem de Esperança para o mundo: Acontecimento e significado de Fátima*. Fatima: Shrine of Fatima, 2012, p. 51-110.

_____ *A Mensagem de Fátima*. 2nd ed. Fatima: Shrine of Fatima, 2014.

Conferência Episcopal Portuguesa – Fátima, sinal de esperança para o nosso tempo. Torres Novas: Gráfica Almondina, 2016.

CRISTINO, Luciano – As aparições de Fátima: reconstituição a partir dos documentos, Fatima: Shrine of Fatima, 2017.

_____ Francisco Marto: percurso de uma vida breve. In Arnaldo de Pinho e Vitor Coutinho, (coord.) *Francisco Marto: Crescer para o Dom*. Fatima: Shrine of Fatima, 2010.

DANIEL DUARTE, Marco; Vazão, Sónia – O Segredo de Fátima. uma cronologia "in fieri". In GOMES Pedro Valinho (coord.). *Segredo: liturgia de Palavra, silêncio e testemunho. Aproximações polissémicas ao segredo de Fátima*. Fatima: Shrine of Fatima, 2018, p. 19-54.

DE FIORES, Stefano – O segredo de Fátima. In COUTINHO, Vítor (coord.). *Mensagem de Esperança para o mundo: Acontecimento e significado de Fátima.* Fatima: Shrine of Fatima, 2012, p. 115-145.

_____ Consagração. In José Carlos Carvalho (coord.). *A Consagração como dedicação na Mensagem de Fátima.* Fatima: Shrine of Fatima, 2014, p. 129-172.

FARIA, Daniel – Dos Líquidos. In *Poesia,* Assírio e Alvim: Lisbon, 2019.

CATHOLIC CHURCH. Congregation for the Doctrine of Faith, Prefect, 1981-2005 (Joseph Ratzinger) – Theological Commentary. In The Message of Fatima. Vatican City: Libreria Editrice Vaticana, 2000. p. 31-43.

_____ Pope, 1978-2005 (John Paul II) – Fátima: l'omelia durante la Santa Messa di Beatificazione Dinanzi al Santuario Mariano di Nostra Signora del Rosario: «La Chiesa pone sul lucerniere i Pastorelli Francesco e Giacinta, due fiamelle che Dio ha acceso per illuminare l'umanità nelle sue ore buie e inquiete»: Sabato 13 maggio. In *Insegnamenti di Giovanni Paolo II.* Vol. XXIII, 1 2000 (gennaio-giugno). Città del Vaticano: Libreria Editrice Vaticana, 2000. p. 837-842.

_____ Pope, 2005-2013 (Benedict XVI) – Iter Apostolicum in Lusitaniam: Dum eucharistica celebratio habetur in área Sanctuarii Dominae Nostrae Fatimensis [2010/05/13]. In *Acta Apostolicae Sedis.* Vol. CII: n. 6 (2010/06/04). Vaticano: Typis Polyglottis Vaticanis, 2010. p. 324-327.

_____ Pope, 2013 - … (Francis) – Homily of the Holy Father[2017/05/13]. In http://www.vatican.va/content/francesco/en/homilies/2017/documents/ papa-francesco_20170513_omelia-pellegrinaggio-fatima._html 12.06.2020 12:50.

JACINTO FARIAS, José – O Coração de Maria e a mística da reparação. *Didaskalia*. Lisbon: Universidade Católica Editora. 47:1 (2017) 203-237.

MANZI, Franco – *As crianças-profetas de Fátima: o olhar de três crianças sobre os Ressuscitados*. Fatima: Shrine of Fatima, 2018.

MARTO, António – Fátima: uma luz sobre a história do mundo. In COUTINHO, Vítor (coord.). *Mensagem de Esperança para o mundo: Acontecimento e significado de Fátima*. Fatima: Shrine of Fatima, 2012, p. 15-46.

PINHO, Arnaldo – Importância e significado das aparições de Fátima. In COUTINHO, Vítor (coord.). *Mensagem de Esperança para o mundo: Acontecimento e significado de Fátima*. Fatima: Shrine of Fatima, 2012, p. 321-343.

PINHO TEIXEIRA, João António – Um coração em trespasse na Cruz. *Didaskalia*. Lisbon: Universidade Católica Editora. 47:1 (2017) 127-161.

RAHNER, Karl – A consagração a Maria nas Congregações marianas. In José Carlos Carvalho (coord.). *A Consagração como dedicação na Mensagem de Fátima*. Fatima: Shrine of Fatima, 2014, p. 99-128.

SCHEFFCZYK, Leo – A mensagem de Paz. In COUTINHO, Vítor (coord.). *Mensagem de Esperança para o mundo: Acontecimento e significado de Fátima.* Fatima: Shrine of Fatima, 2012, p. 243-315.